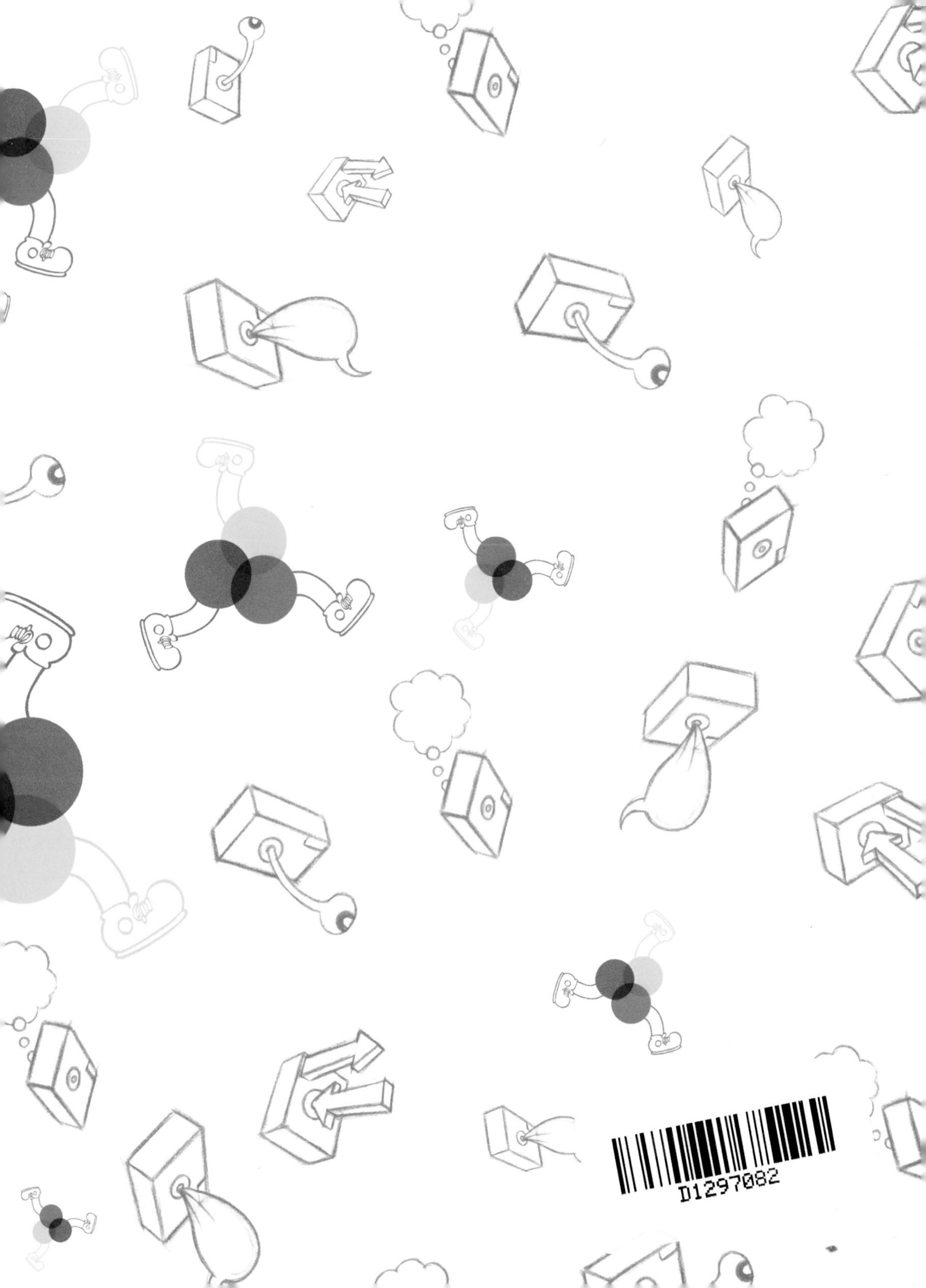

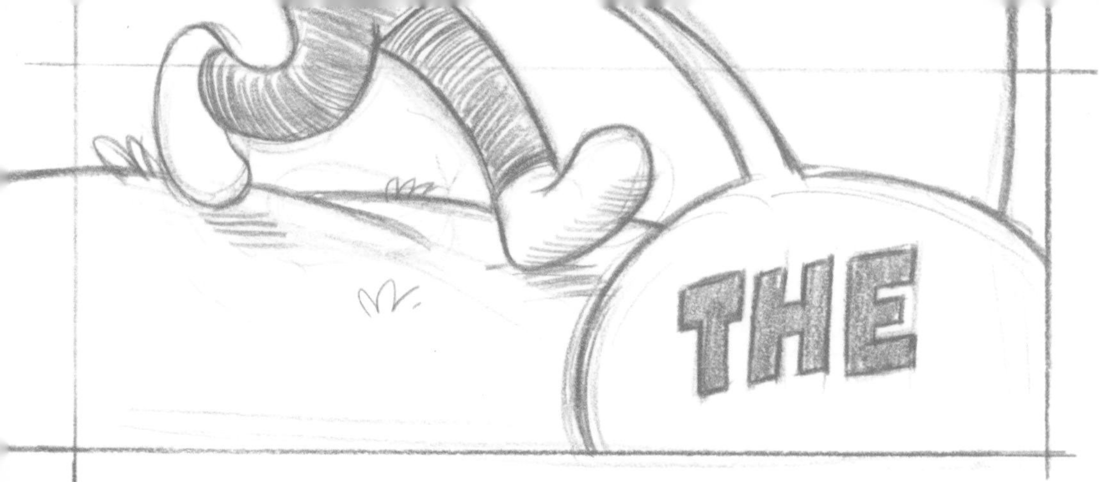
THE

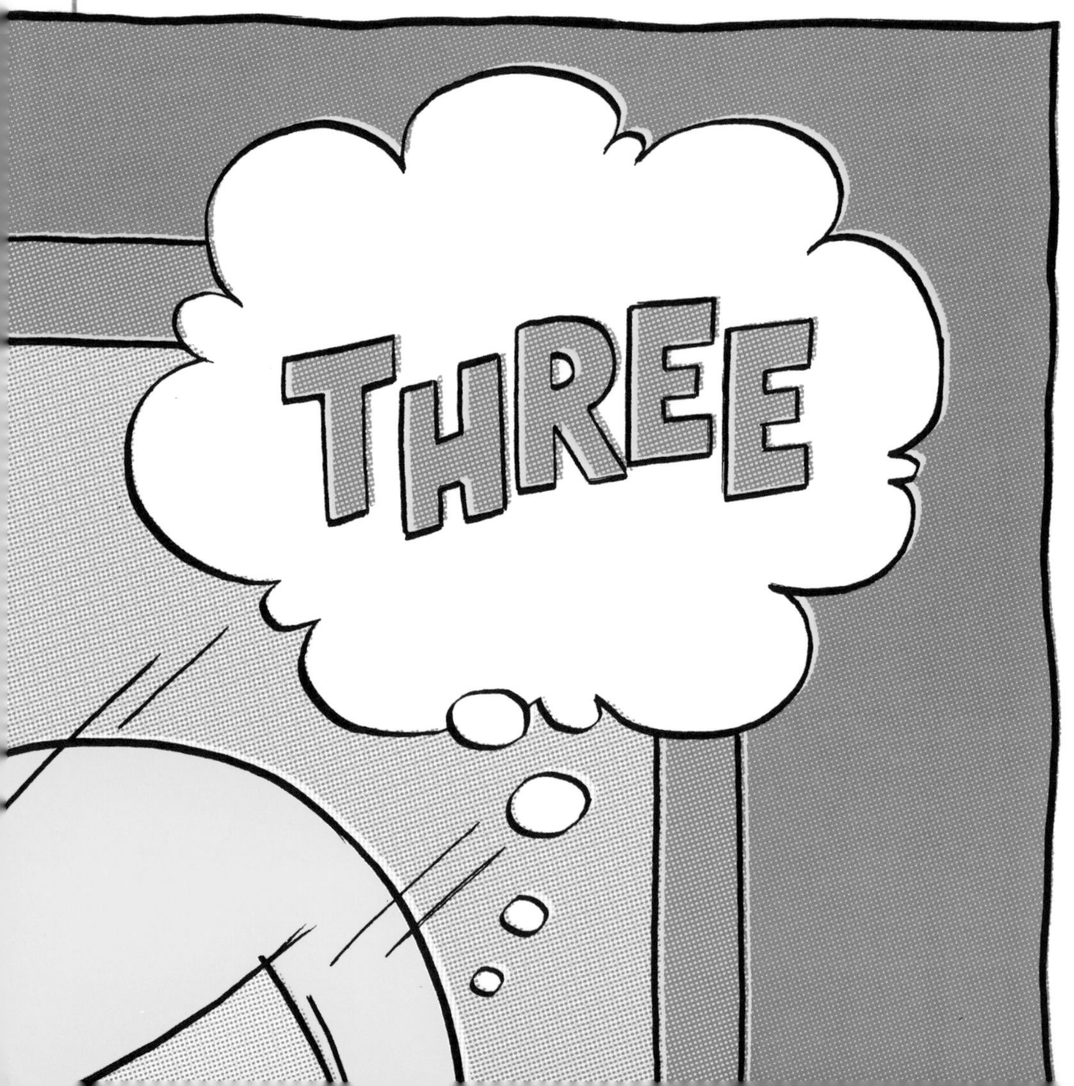
THREE

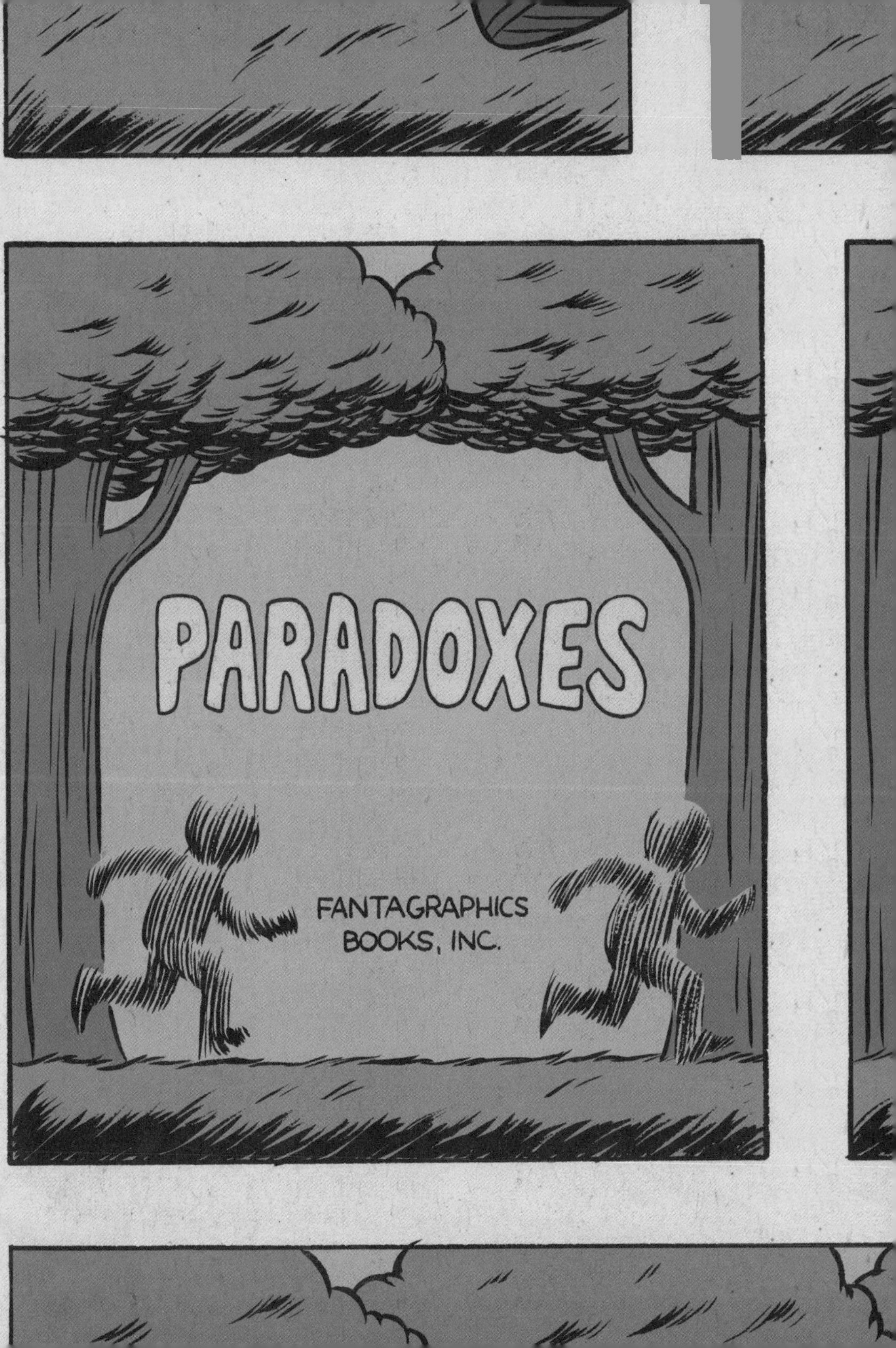
PARADOXES
FANTAGRAPHICS BOOKS, INC.

CONCERNING THE READING OF THIS VOLUME:

1. "JULIANE" - A GERMANIC NAME - IS PRONOUNCED YOU-LEE-AH-NUH.

2. DESPITE STATEMENTS ELSEWHERE IN THIS VOLUME, THERE ARE THOSE WHO WILL QUESTION THIS VOLUME'S TRUTH AND/OR ACCURACY. TO THIS END, THE AUTHOR SUBMITS THE FOLLOWING EXPERT STATEMENT

> "IF YOU CAN'T BELIEVE WHAT YOU READ IN THE COMIC BOOKS, WHAT CAN YOU BELIEVE?"
>
> -BULLWINKLE J. MOOSE
> (THE WAILING WHALE, EPISODE ONE)

3. THE AUTHOR'S YOUNGER SISTER HAS POINTED OUT THAT OHIO IS NOT AS ALTOGETHER FLAT AS PAGE TWELVE OF THIS VOLUME WOULD IMPLY. DULY CONCEDED.

4. THE AUTHOR'S ELDER SISTER HAS FIELDED INNUMERABLE QUESTIONS FROM THE AUTHOR REGARDING THE INTERSECTION OF HER EXPERTISE AND THIS VOLUME'S CONTENT. DULY APPRECIATED.

PUBLISHED BY GARY GROTH
AND KIM THOMPSON
PROMOTION BY ERIC REYNOLDS
BOOK DESIGN BY THE AUTHOR

ISBN 978-1-56097-653-0

PRINTED IN SINGAPORE

FIRST EDITION: APRIL 2007

THE THREE PARADOXES. PUBLISHED BY FANTAGRAPHICS BOOKS 7563 LAKE CITY WAY NE, SEATTLE, WA 98115 WWW.FANTAGRAPHICS.COM.

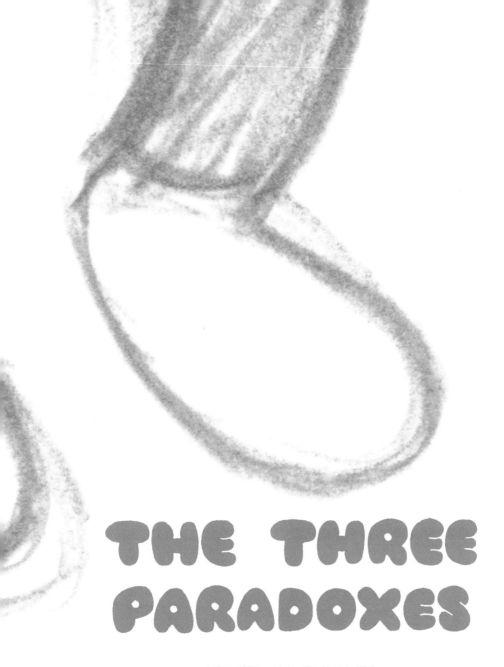

THE THREE PARADOXES

WRITTEN AND DRAWN BY
PAUL HORNSCHEMEIER

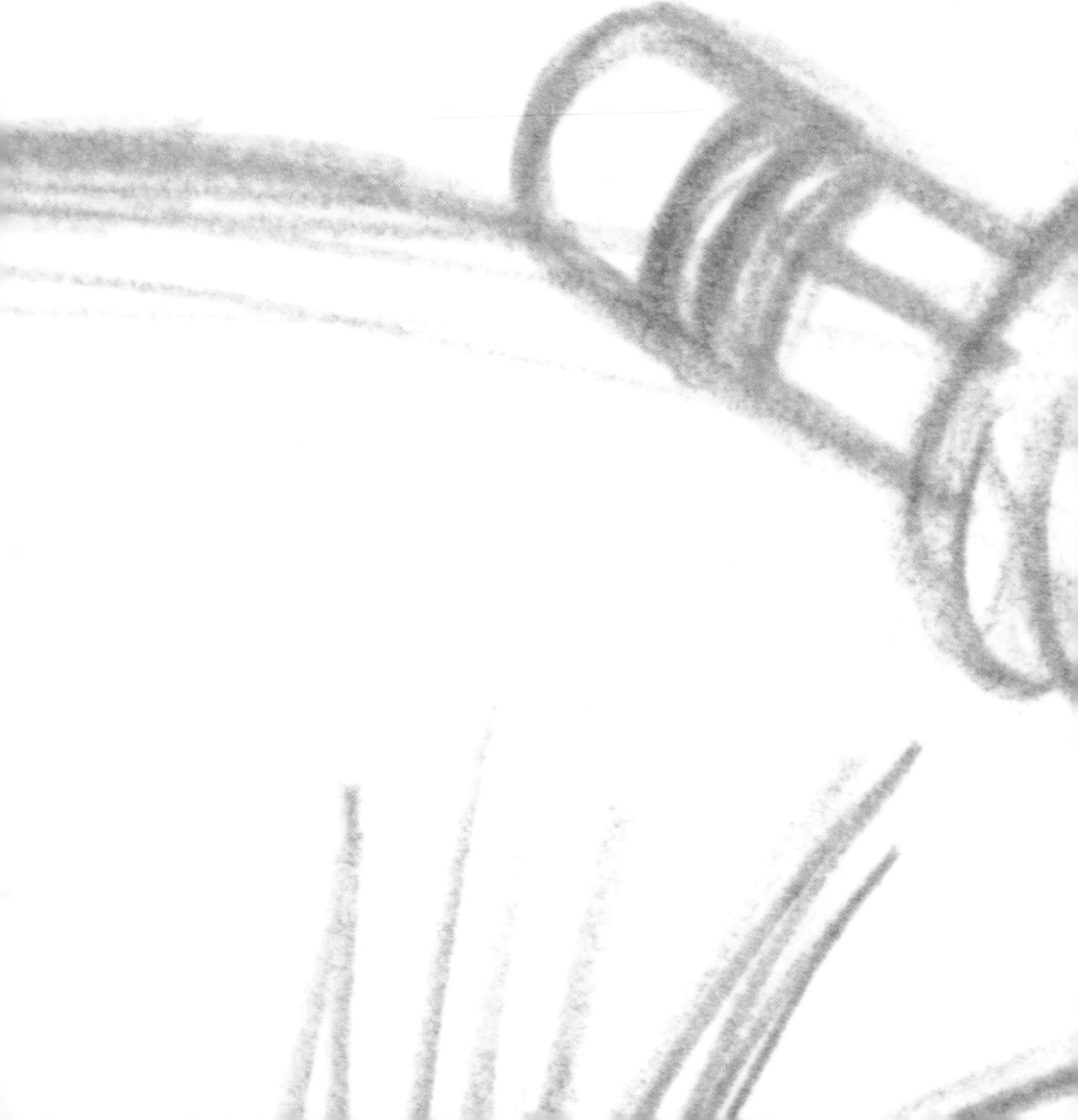

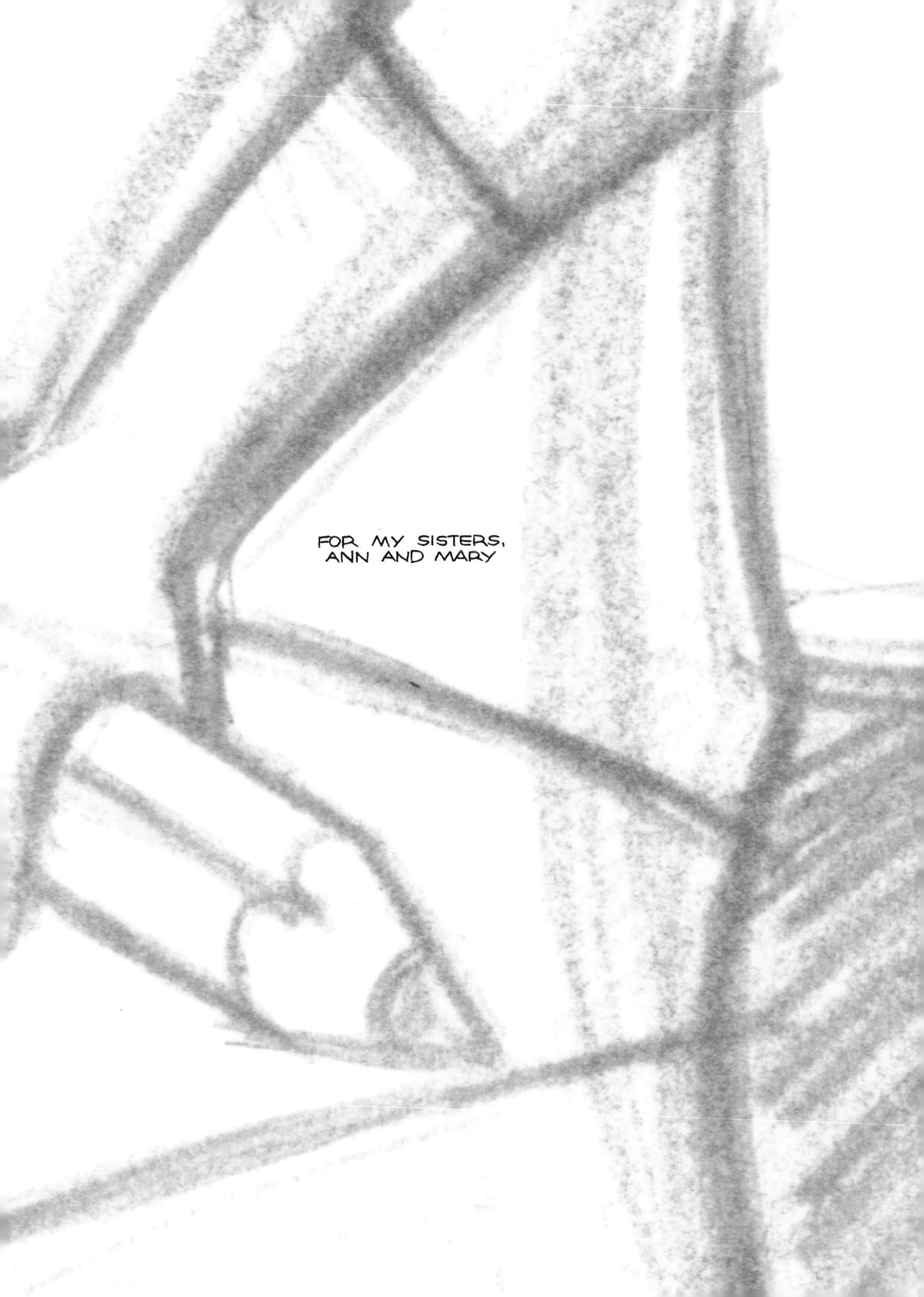

FOR MY SISTERS,
ANN AND MARY

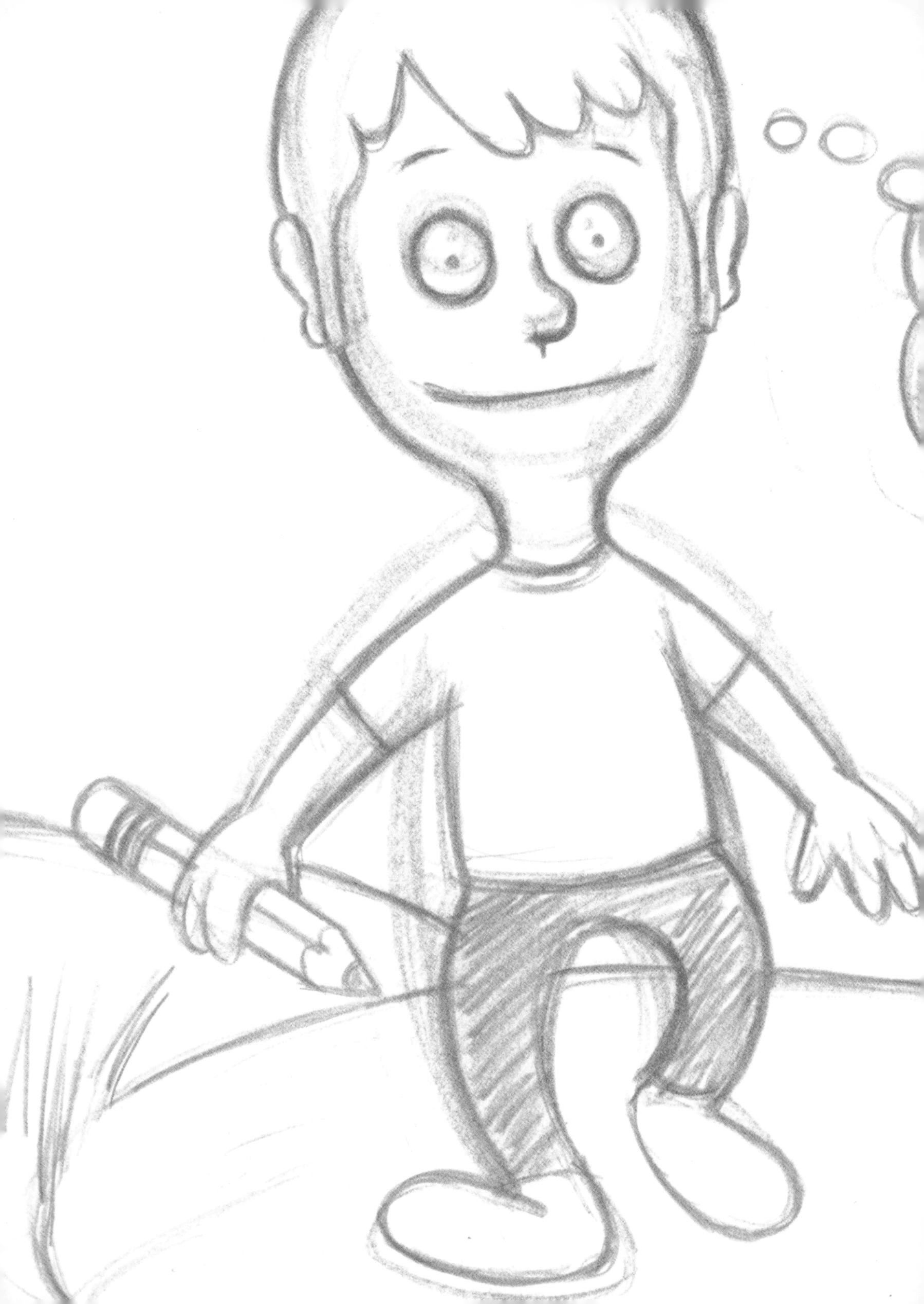

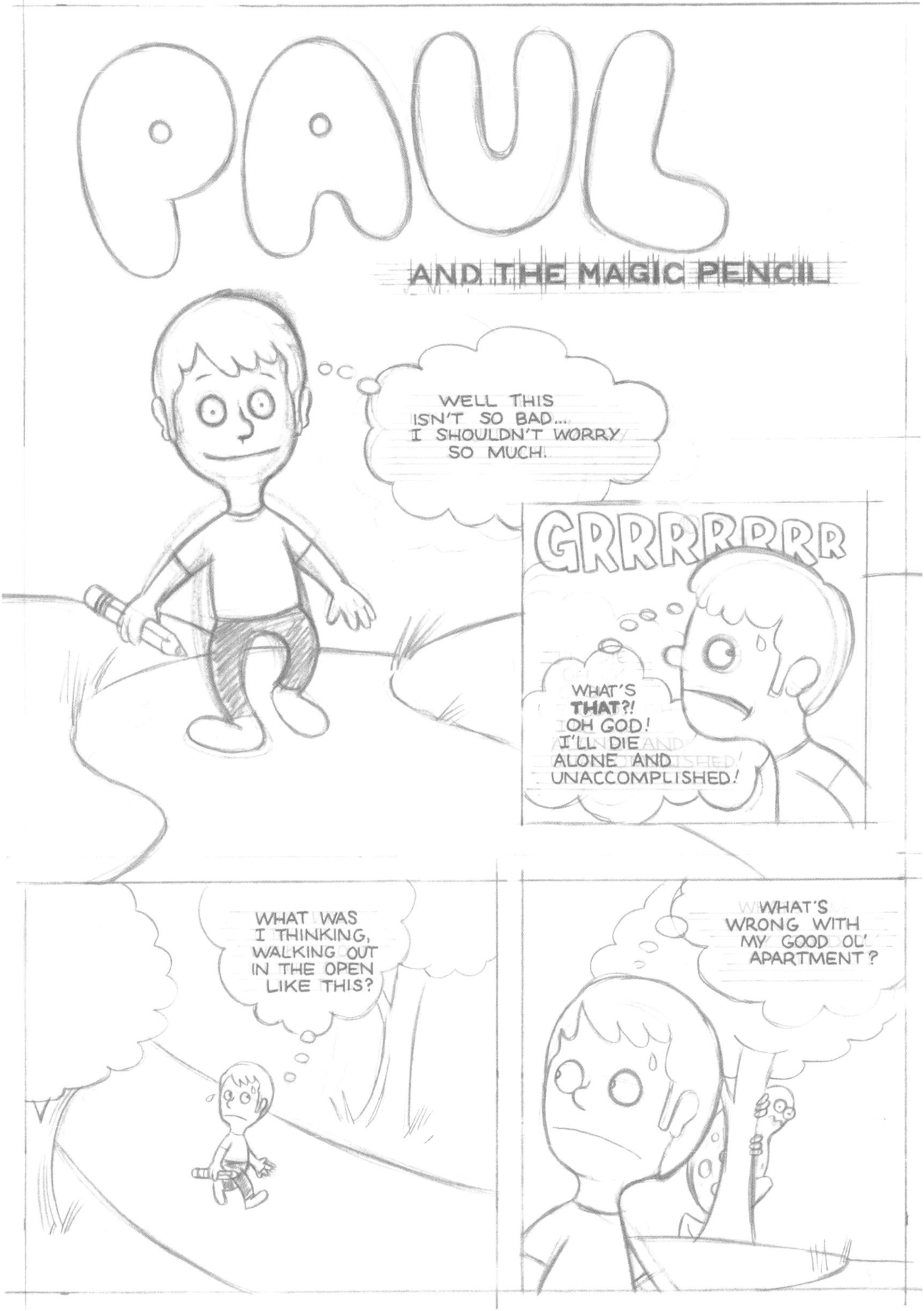
PAUL
AND THE MAGIC PENCIL
WELL THIS ISN'T SO BAD... I SHOULDN'T WORRY SO MUCH.
GRRRRRRR
WHAT'S **THAT**?! OH GOD! I'LL DIE ALONE AND UNACCOMPLISHED!
WHAT WAS I THINKING, WALKING OUT IN THE OPEN LIKE THIS?
WHAT'S WRONG WITH MY GOOD OL' APARTMENT?

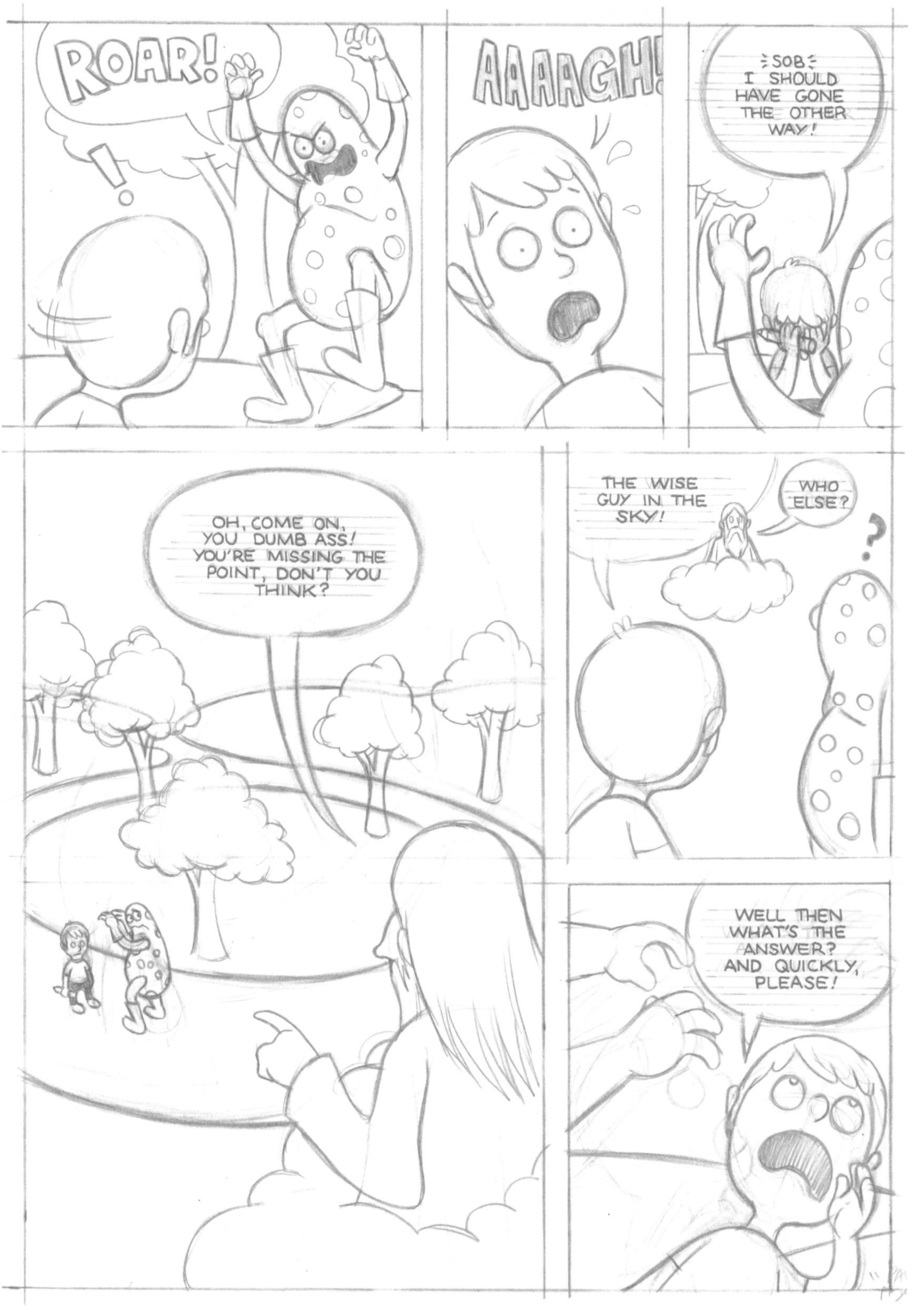
ROAR!
!
AAAAGH!
SOB
I SHOULD HAVE GONE THE OTHER WAY!
OH, COME ON, YOU DUMB ASS! YOU'RE MISSING THE POINT, DON'T YOU THINK?
THE WISE GUY IN THE SKY!
WHO ELSE?
?
WELL THEN WHAT'S THE ANSWER? AND QUICKLY, PLEASE!

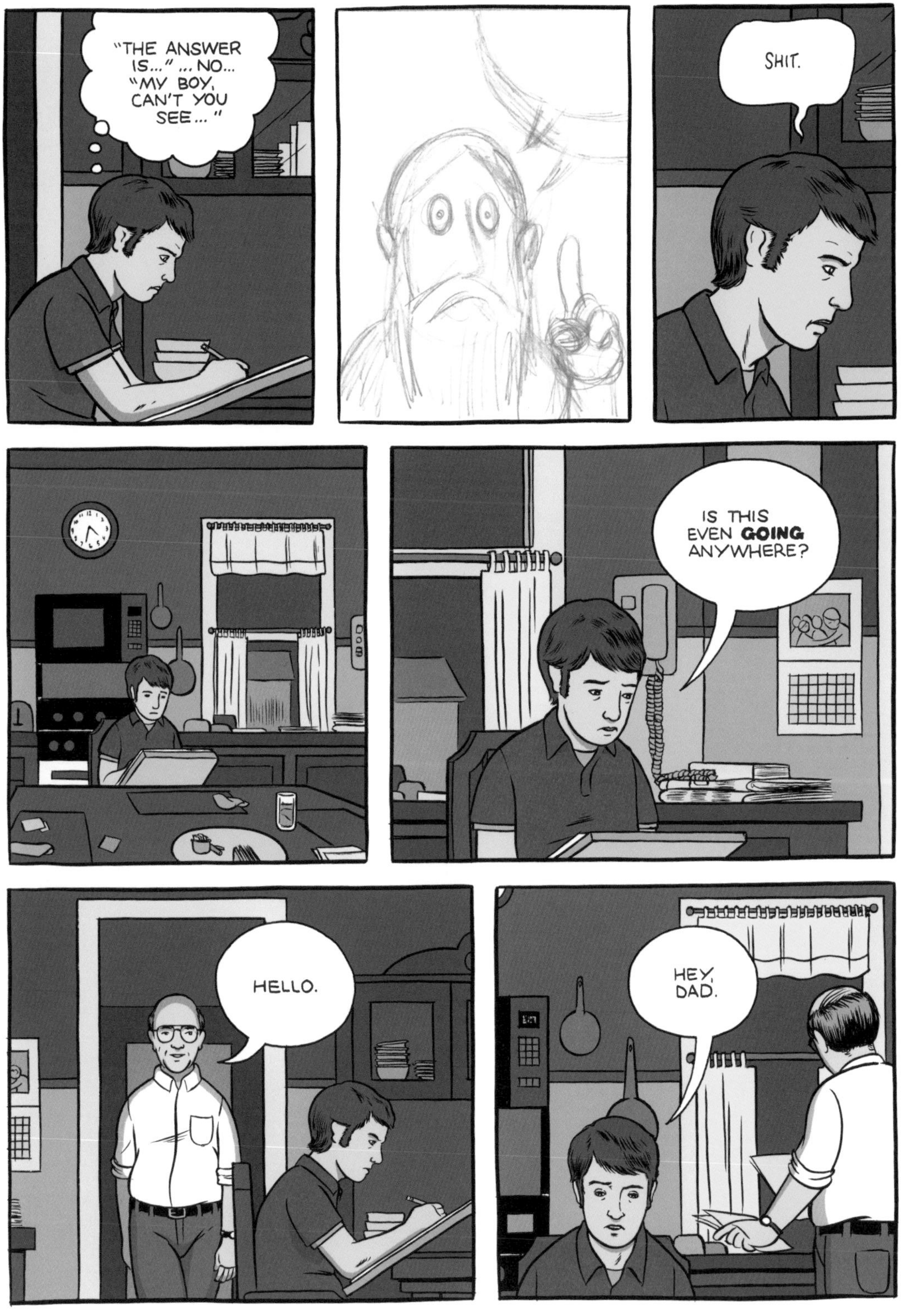
"THE ANSWER IS..." ...NO... "MY BOY, CAN'T YOU SEE..."
SHIT.
IS THIS EVEN **GOING** ANYWHERE?
HELLO.
HEY, DAD.

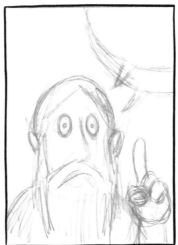

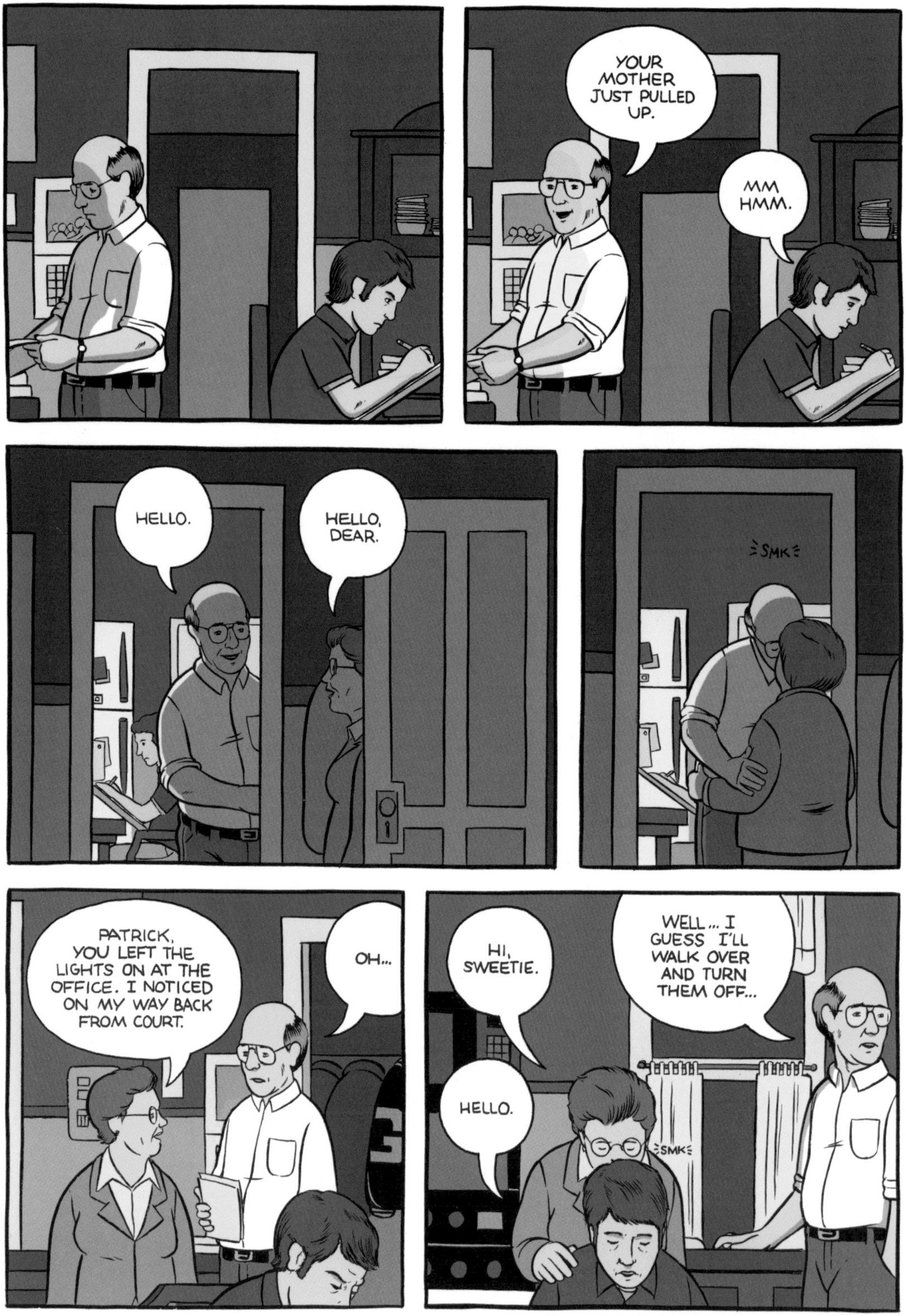
YOUR MOTHER JUST PULLED UP.
MM HMM.
HELLO.
HELLO, DEAR.
SMK
PATRICK, YOU LEFT THE LIGHTS ON AT THE OFFICE. I NOTICED ON MY WAY BACK FROM COURT.
OH...
HI, SWEETIE.
WELL... I GUESS I'LL WALK OVER AND TURN THEM OFF...
HELLO.
SMK

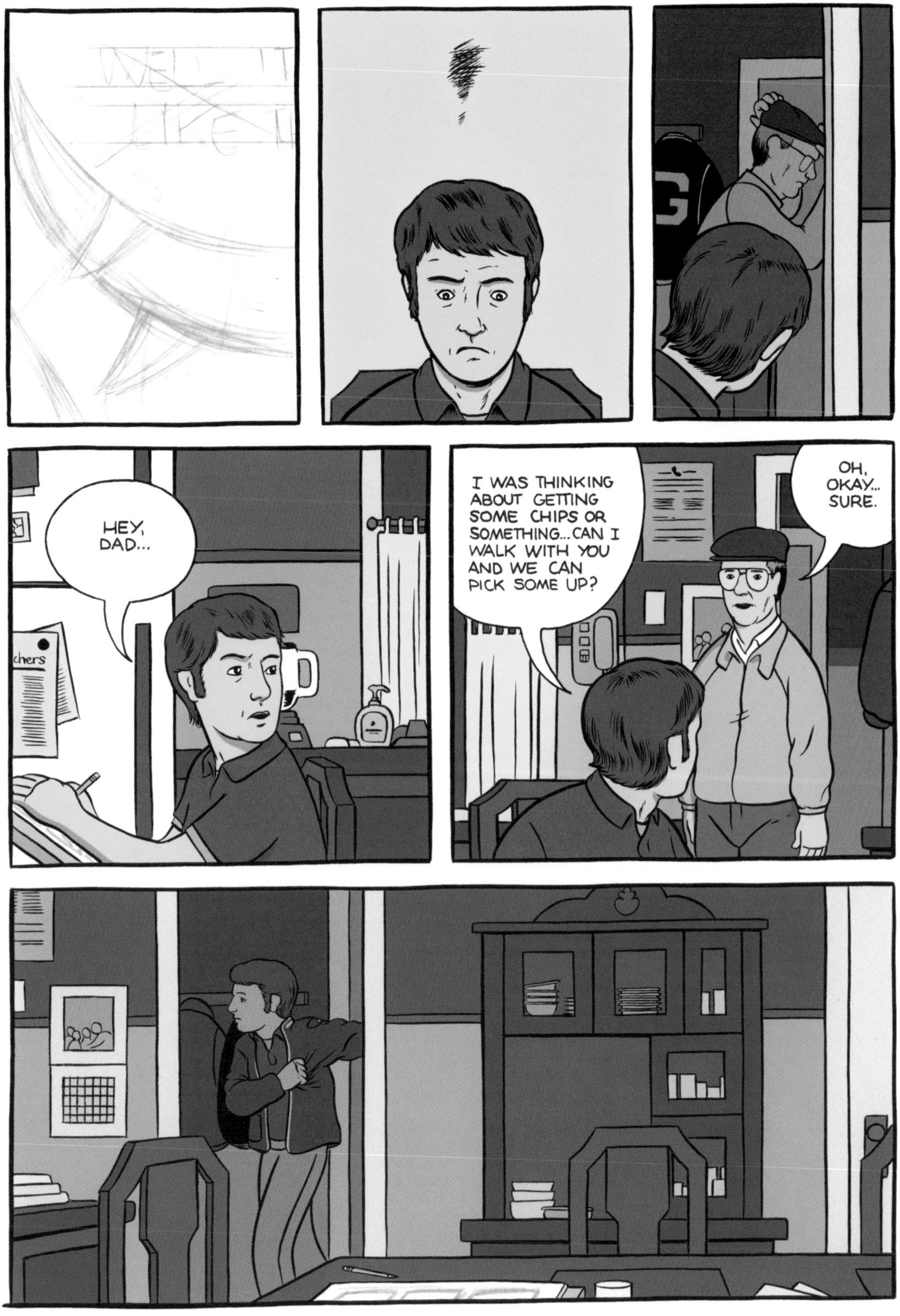
HEY, DAD...
I WAS THINKING ABOUT GETTING SOME CHIPS OR SOMETHING...CAN I WALK WITH YOU AND WE CAN PICK SOME UP?
OH, OKAY... SURE.

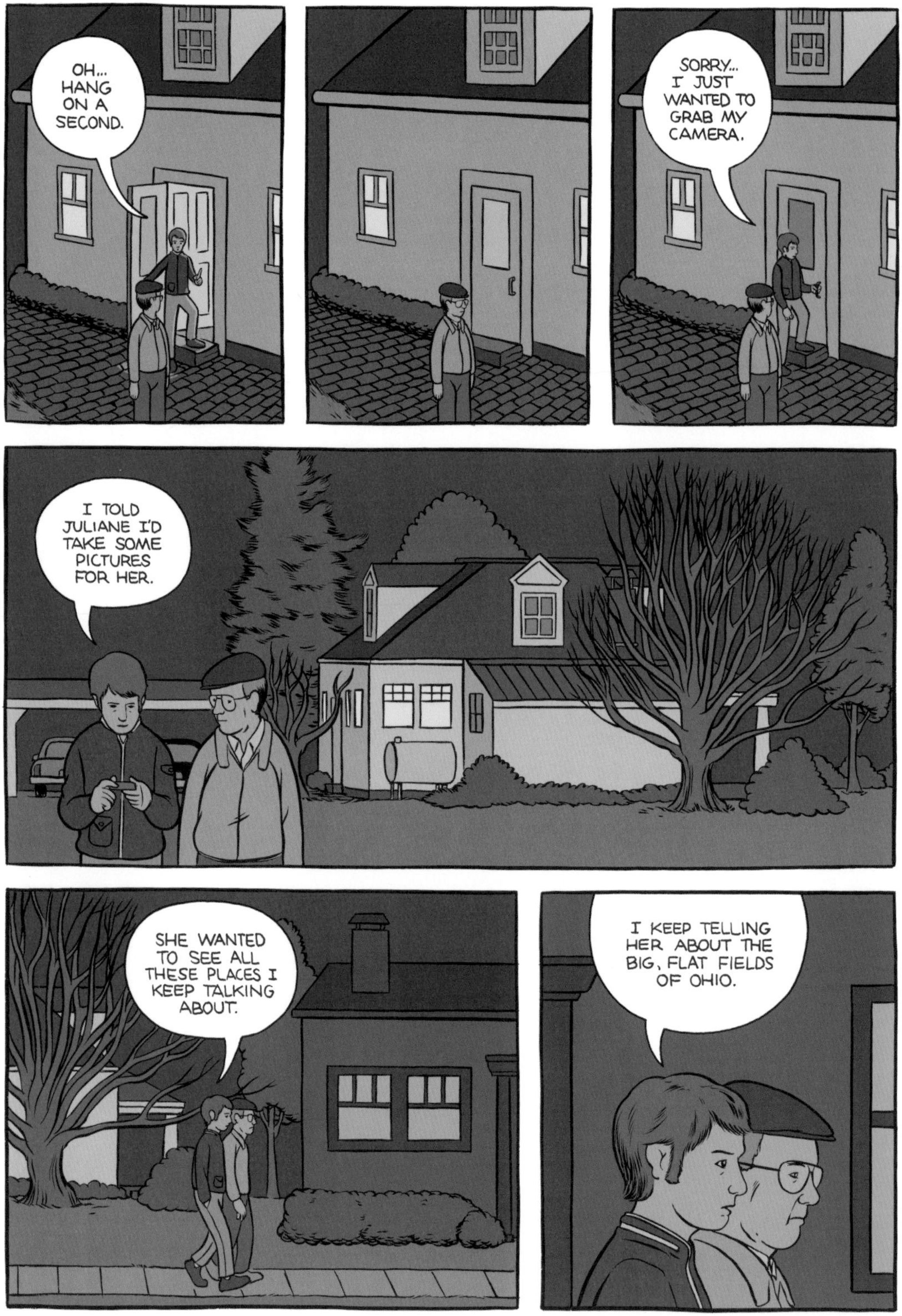
OH... HANG ON A SECOND.
SORRY... I JUST WANTED TO GRAB MY CAMERA.
I TOLD JULIANE I'D TAKE SOME PICTURES FOR HER.
SHE WANTED TO SEE ALL THESE PLACES I KEEP TALKING ABOUT.
I KEEP TELLING HER ABOUT THE BIG, FLAT FIELDS OF OHIO.

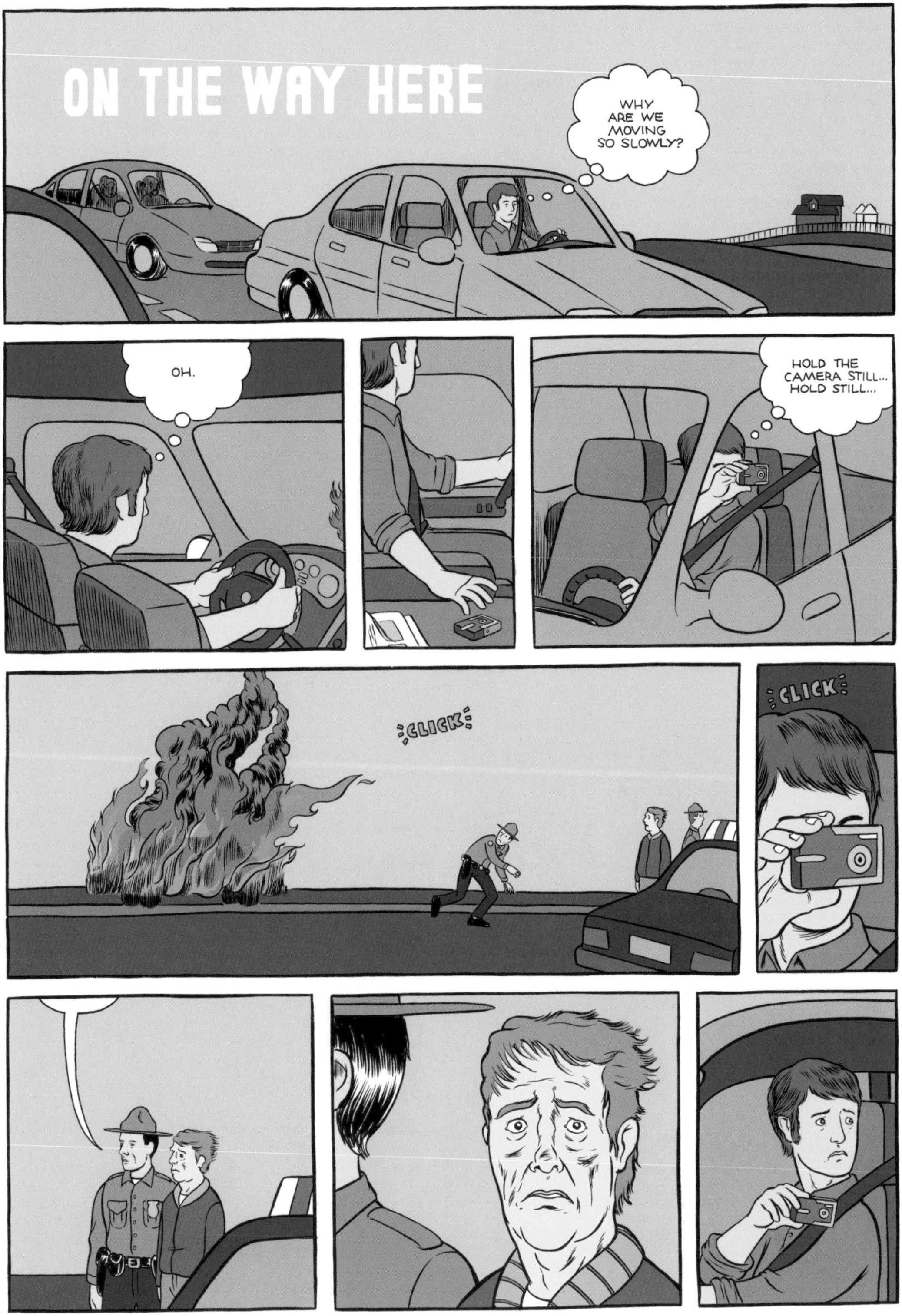
ON THE WAY HERE
WHY ARE WE MOVING SO SLOWLY?
OH.
HOLD THE CAMERA STILL... HOLD STILL...
CLICK
CLICK

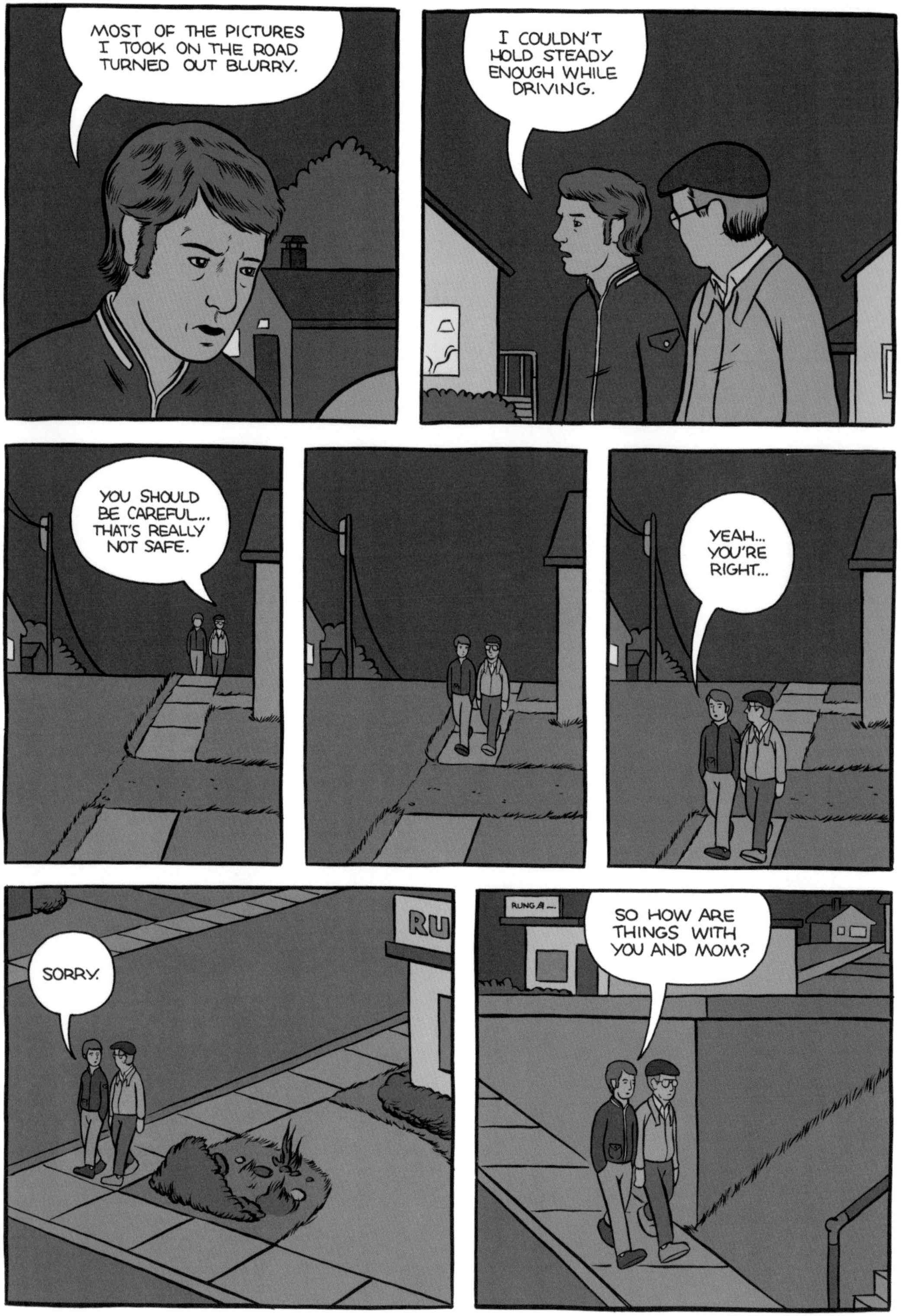
MOST OF THE PICTURES I TOOK ON THE ROAD TURNED OUT BLURRY.
I COULDN'T HOLD STEADY ENOUGH WHILE DRIVING.
YOU SHOULD BE CAREFUL... THAT'S REALLY NOT SAFE.
YEAH... YOU'RE RIGHT...
RU
SORRY.
RUNG
SO HOW ARE THINGS WITH YOU AND MOM?

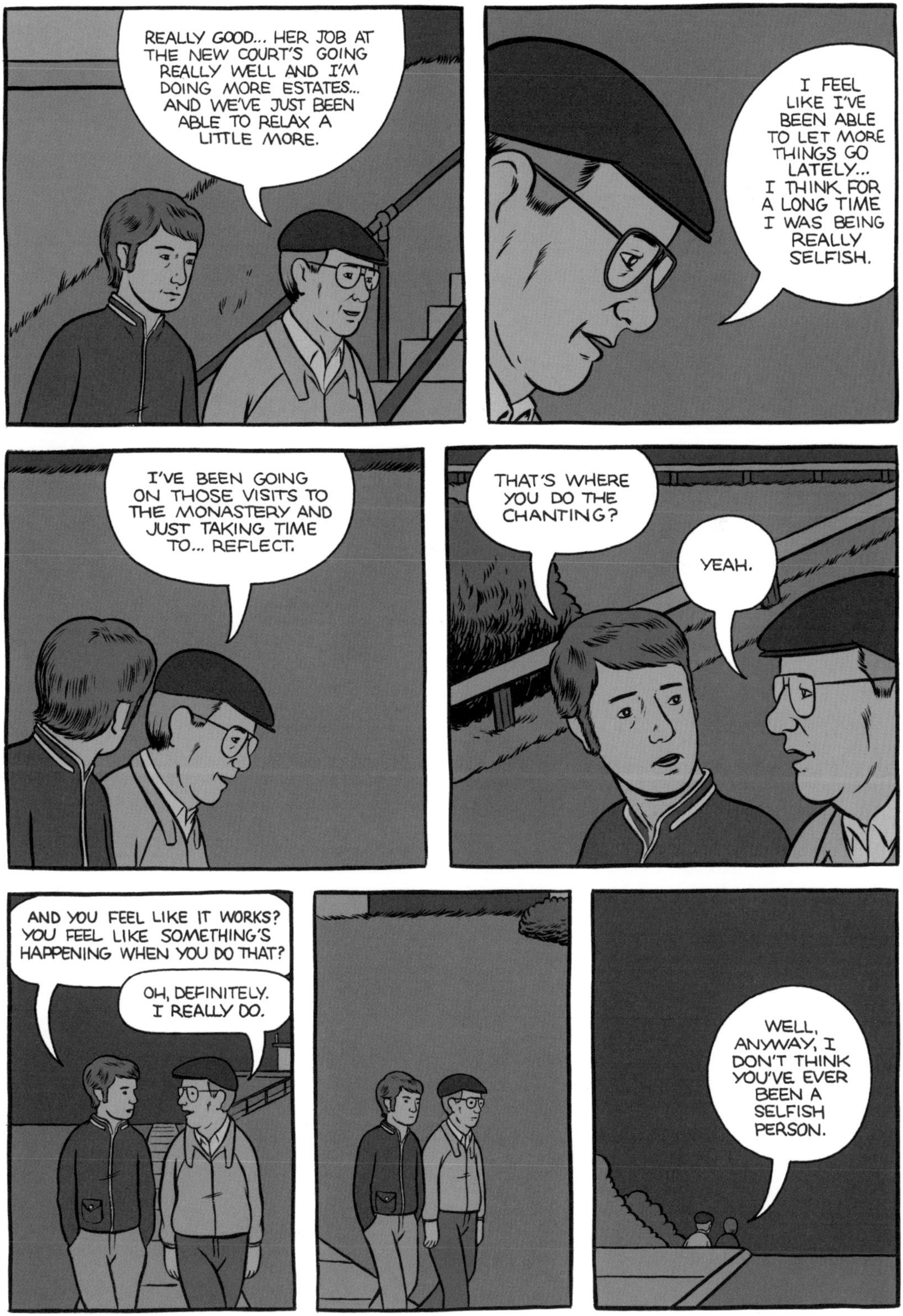
REALLY GOOD... HER JOB AT THE NEW COURT'S GOING REALLY WELL AND I'M DOING MORE ESTATES... AND WE'VE JUST BEEN ABLE TO RELAX A LITTLE MORE.
I FEEL LIKE I'VE BEEN ABLE TO LET MORE THINGS GO LATELY... I THINK FOR A LONG TIME I WAS BEING REALLY SELFISH.
I'VE BEEN GOING ON THOSE VISITS TO THE MONASTERY AND JUST TAKING TIME TO... REFLECT.
THAT'S WHERE YOU DO THE CHANTING?
YEAH.
AND YOU FEEL LIKE IT WORKS? YOU FEEL LIKE SOMETHING'S HAPPENING WHEN YOU DO THAT?
OH, DEFINITELY. I REALLY DO.
WELL, ANYWAY, I DON'T THINK YOU'VE EVER BEEN A SELFISH PERSON.

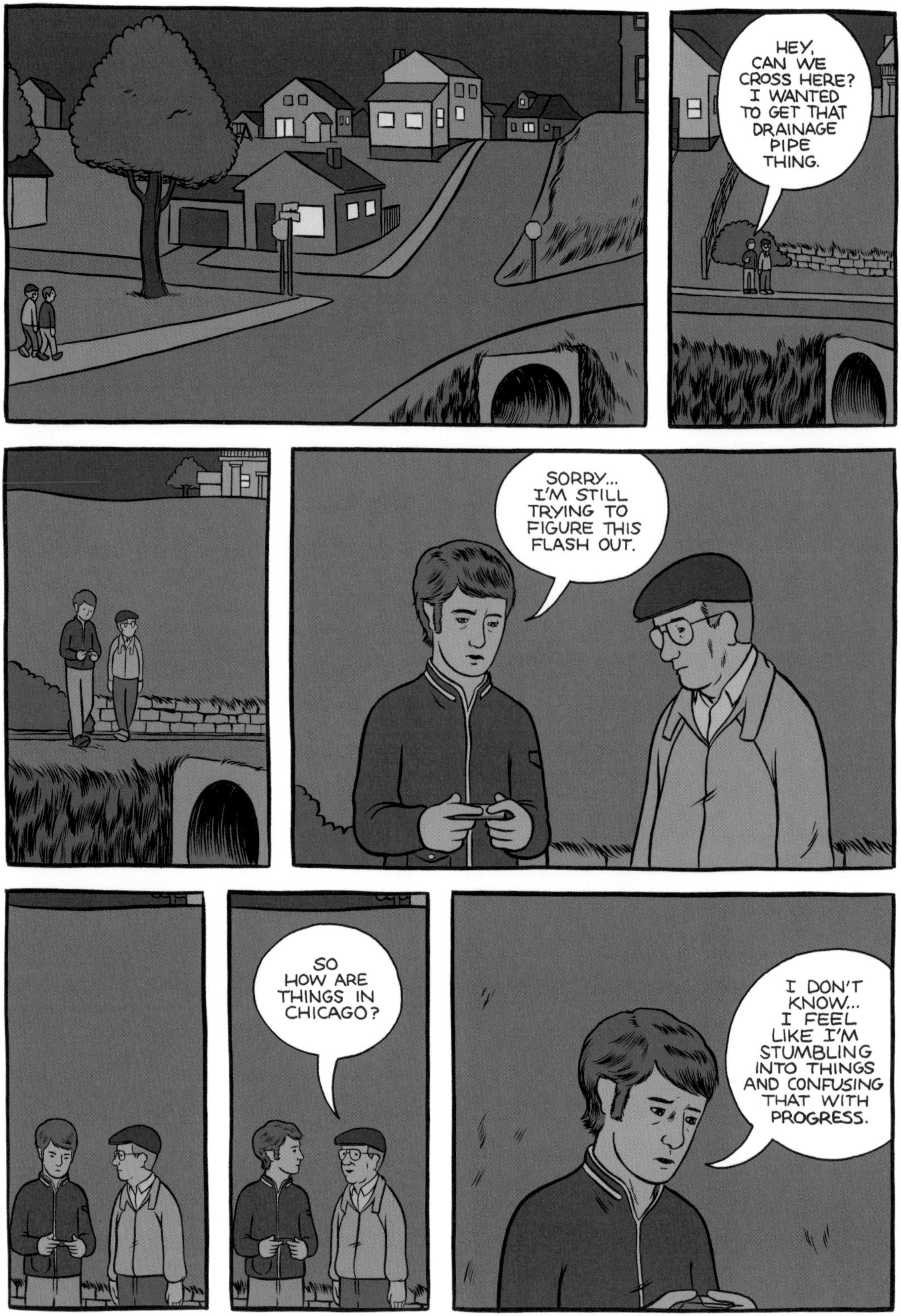
HEY, CAN WE CROSS HERE? I WANTED TO GET THAT DRAINAGE PIPE THING.
SORRY... I'M STILL TRYING TO FIGURE THIS FLASH OUT.
SO HOW ARE THINGS IN CHICAGO?
I DON'T KNOW... I FEEL LIKE I'M STUMBLING INTO THINGS AND CONFUSING THAT WITH PROGRESS.

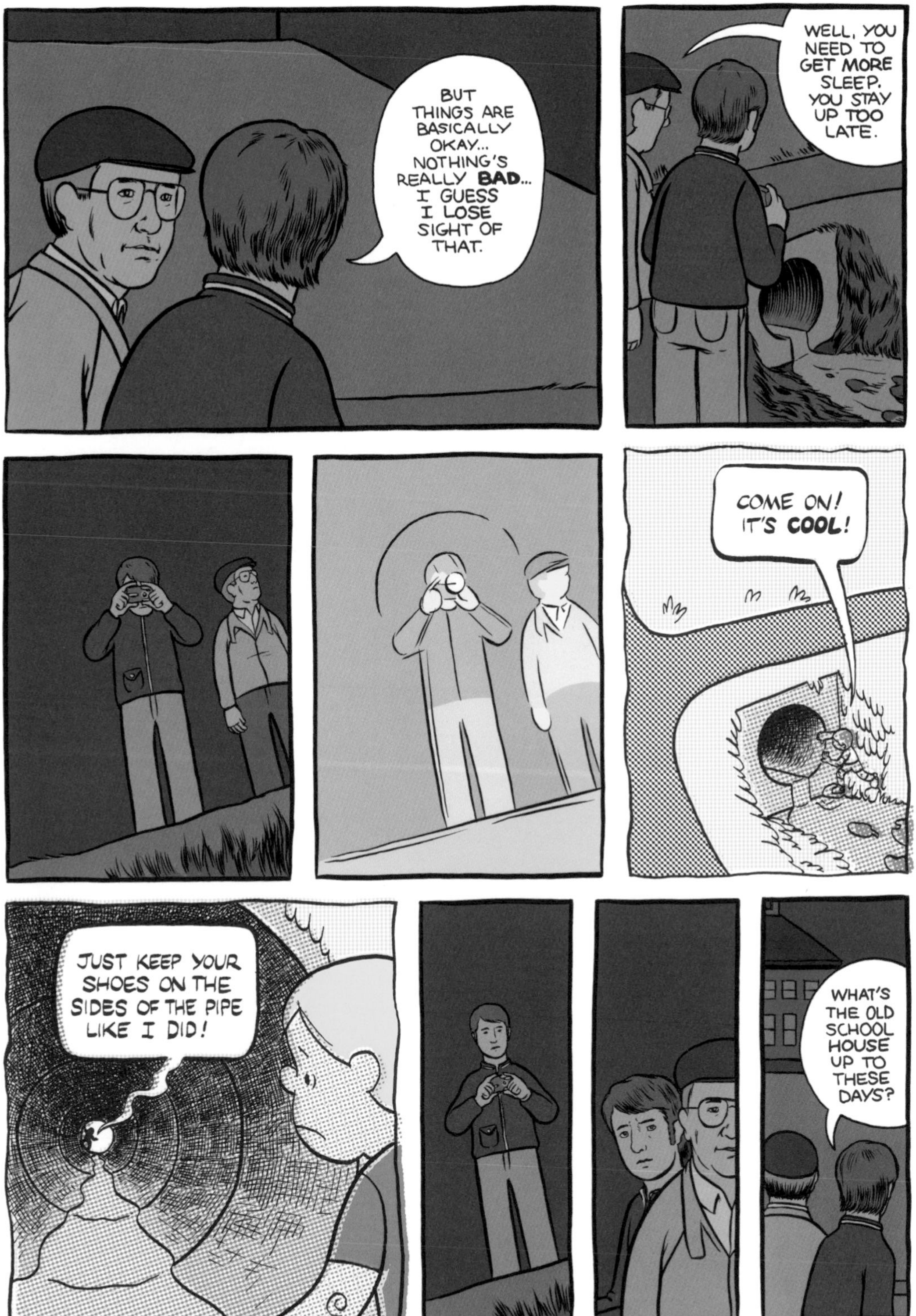
BUT THINGS ARE BASICALLY OKAY... NOTHING'S REALLY BAD... I GUESS I LOSE SIGHT OF THAT.
WELL, YOU NEED TO GET MORE SLEEP. YOU STAY UP TOO LATE.
COME ON! IT'S COOL!
JUST KEEP YOUR SHOES ON THE SIDES OF THE PIPE LIKE I DID!
WHAT'S THE OLD SCHOOL HOUSE UP TO THESE DAYS?

WELL, THERE'S ACTUALLY BEEN SOME DEBATE ABOUT THAT RECENTLY.

DON'T SEE HOW THEY COULD...

WHY...IT WAS ALL MADE OF BUTTER! LOOK AT ALL THIS BUTTER!

IT WAS, OF COURSE, TEMPORARY.

HUH... REALLY?

SO I GUESS IT WAS ALL JUST A BIG MISUNDER-STANDING!

ALL'S WELL THAT FRIENDS WELL!

THE END

TOO WELL

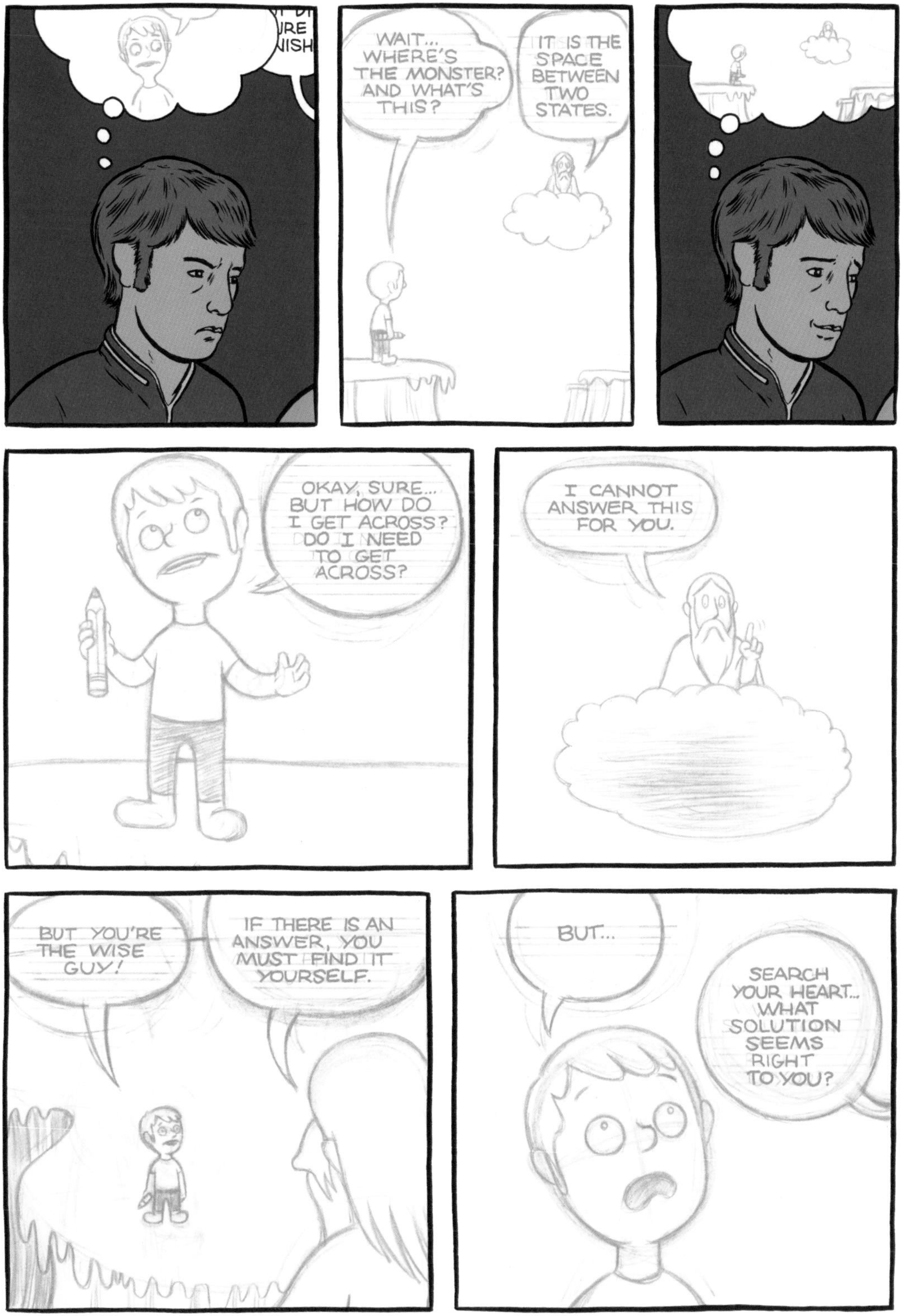
WAIT... WHERE'S THE MONSTER? AND WHAT'S THIS?
IT IS THE SPACE BETWEEN TWO STATES.
OKAY, SURE... BUT HOW DO I GET ACROSS? DO I NEED TO GET ACROSS?
I CANNOT ANSWER THIS FOR YOU.
BUT YOU'RE THE WISE GUY!
IF THERE IS AN ANSWER, YOU MUST FIND IT YOURSELF.
BUT...
SEARCH YOUR HEART... WHAT SOLUTION SEEMS RIGHT TO YOU?

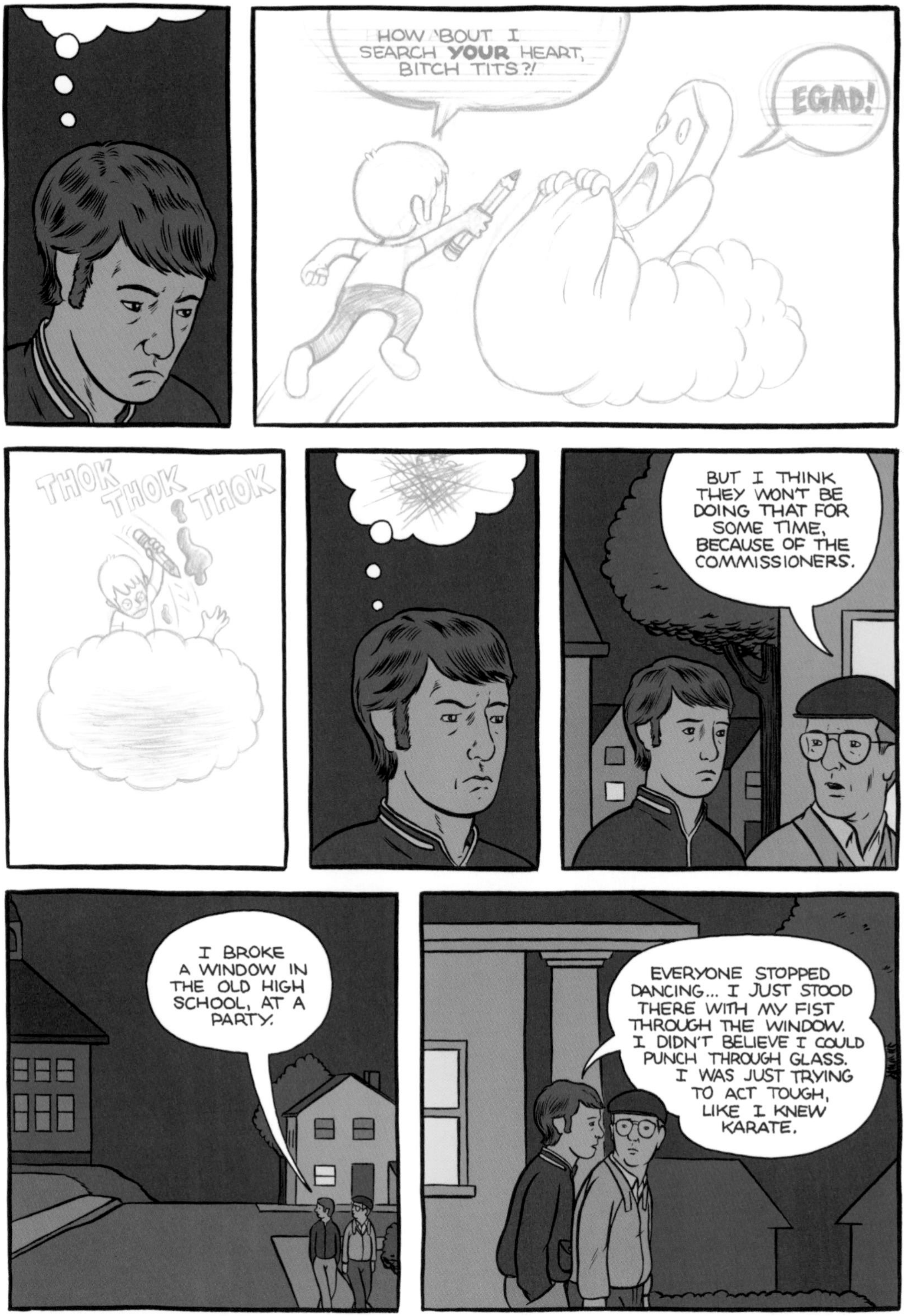
HOW 'BOUT I SEARCH YOUR HEART, BITCH TITS?!
EGAD!
THOK THOK THOK
BUT I THINK THEY WON'T BE DOING THAT FOR SOME TIME, BECAUSE OF THE COMMISSIONERS.
I BROKE A WINDOW IN THE OLD HIGH SCHOOL, AT A PARTY.
EVERYONE STOPPED DANCING... I JUST STOOD THERE WITH MY FIST THROUGH THE WINDOW. I DIDN'T BELIEVE I COULD PUNCH THROUGH GLASS. I WAS JUST TRYING TO ACT TOUGH, LIKE I KNEW KARATE.

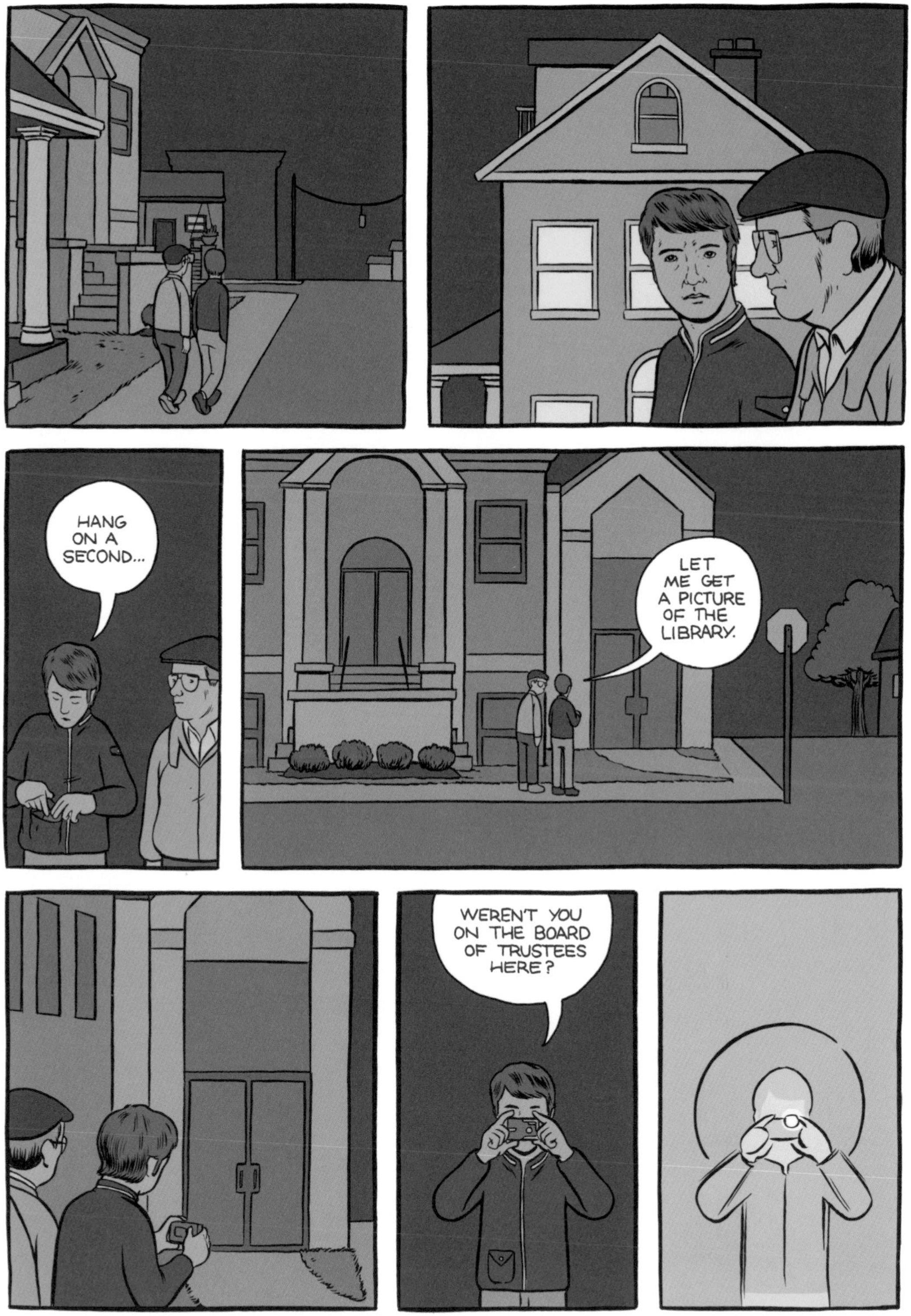
HANG ON A SECOND...
LET ME GET A PICTURE OF THE LIBRARY.
WEREN'T YOU ON THE BOARD OF TRUSTEES HERE?

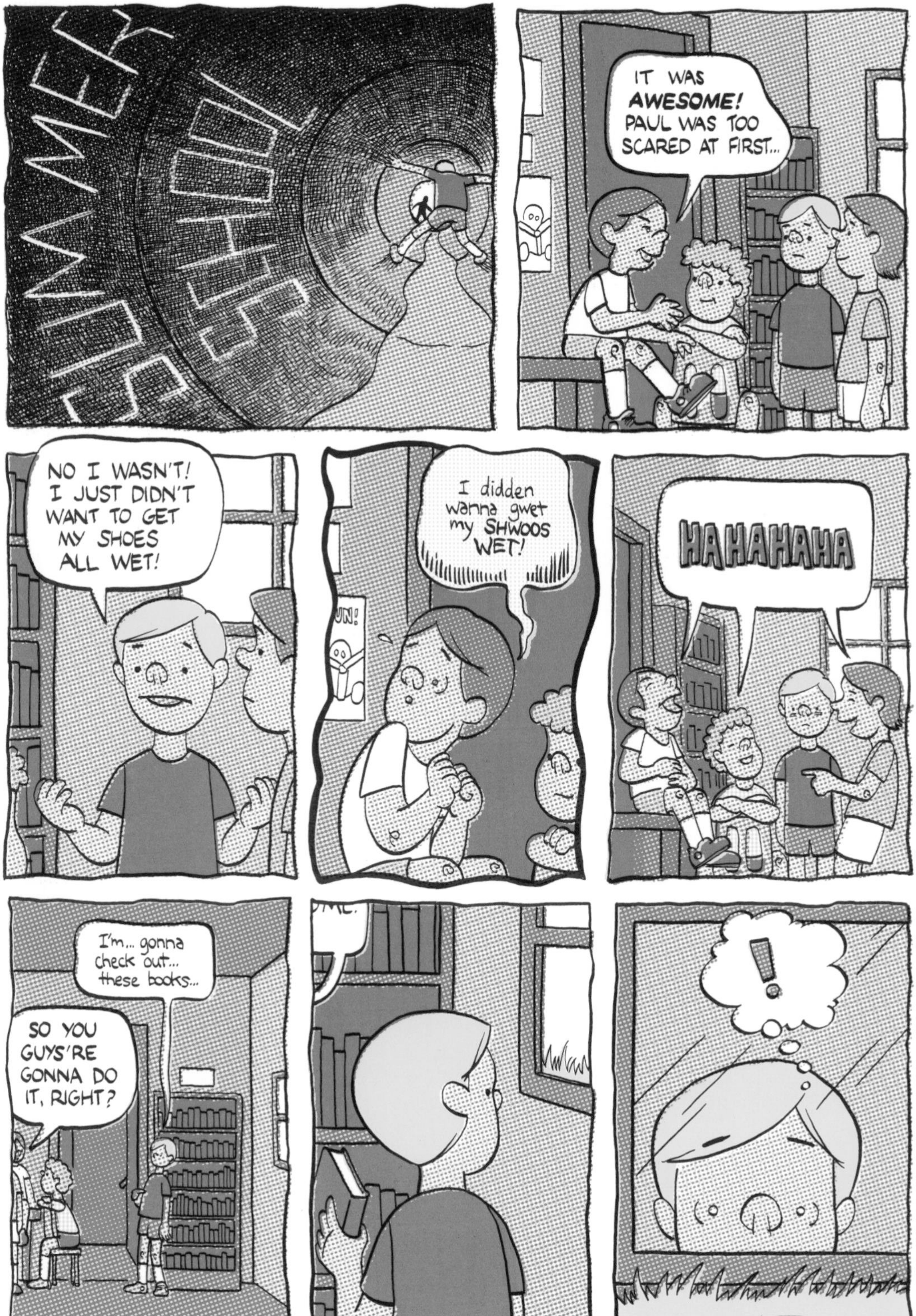
IT WAS **AWESOME!** PAUL WAS TOO SCARED AT FIRST...
NO I WASN'T! I JUST DIDN'T WANT TO GET MY SHOES ALL WET!
I didden wanna gwet my SHWOOS WET!
HAHAHAHA
I'm... gonna check out... these books...
SO YOU GUYS'RE GONNA DO IT, RIGHT?
!

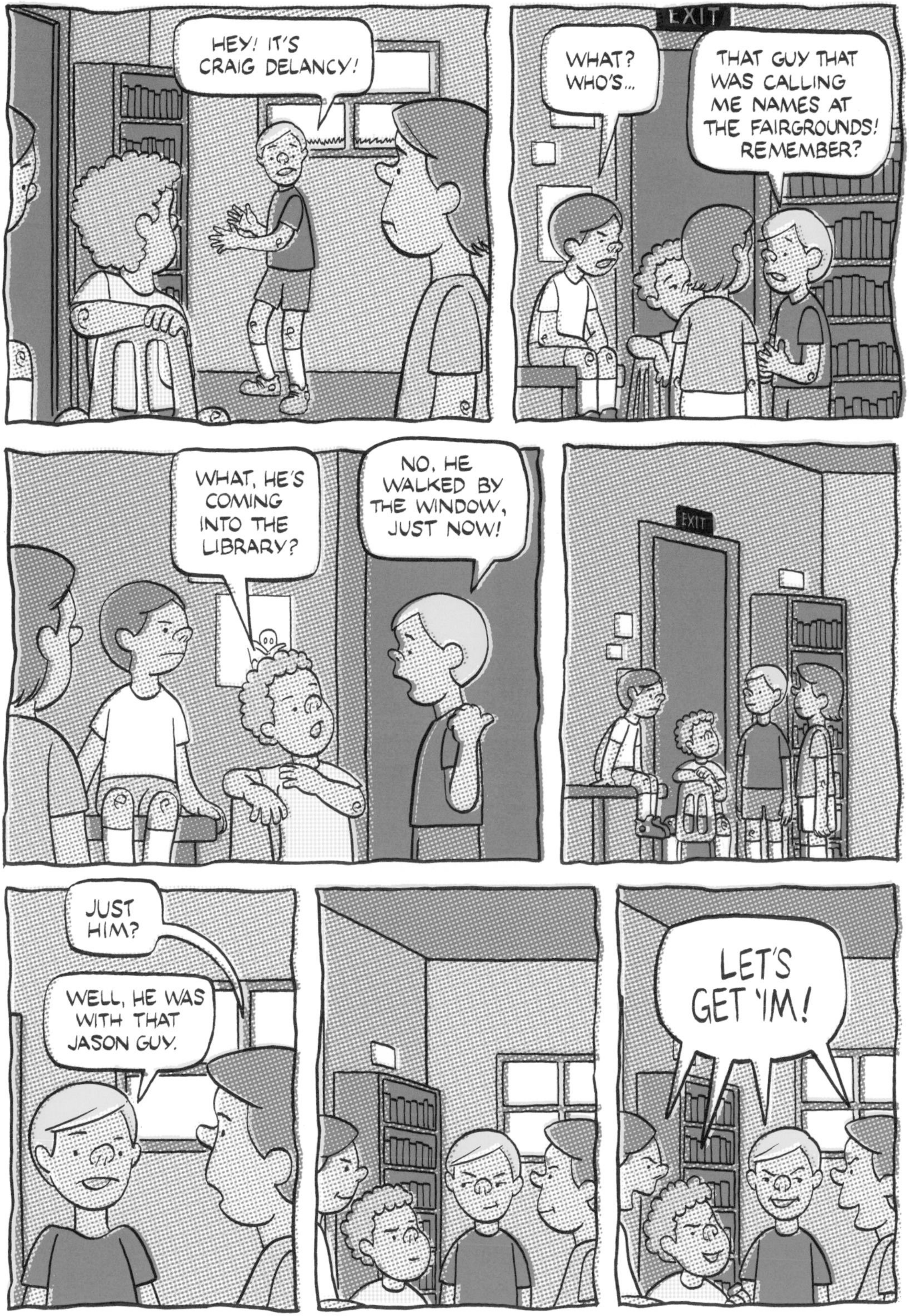
HEY! IT'S CRAIG DELANCY!
EXIT
WHAT? WHO'S...
THAT GUY THAT WAS CALLING ME NAMES AT THE FAIRGROUNDS! REMEMBER?
WHAT, HE'S COMING INTO THE LIBRARY?
NO, HE WALKED BY THE WINDOW, JUST NOW!
EXIT
JUST HIM?
WELL, HE WAS WITH THAT JASON GUY.
LET'S GET 'IM!

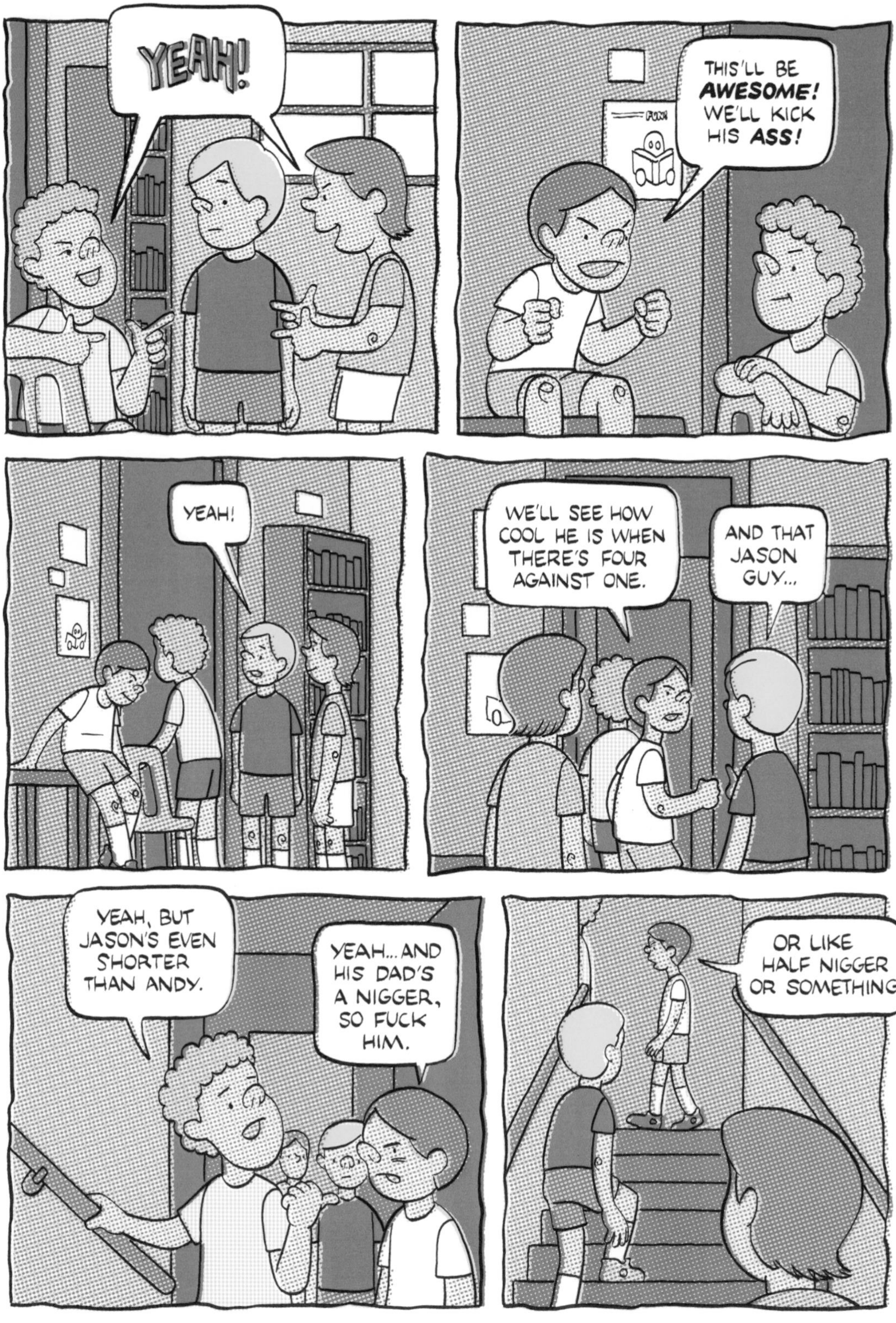
YEAH!
THIS'LL BE AWESOME! WE'LL KICK HIS ASS!
YEAH!
WE'LL SEE HOW COOL HE IS WHEN THERE'S FOUR AGAINST ONE.
AND THAT JASON GUY...
YEAH, BUT JASON'S EVEN SHORTER THAN ANDY.
YEAH... AND HIS DAD'S A NIGGER, SO FUCK HIM.
OR LIKE HALF NIGGER OR SOMETHING.

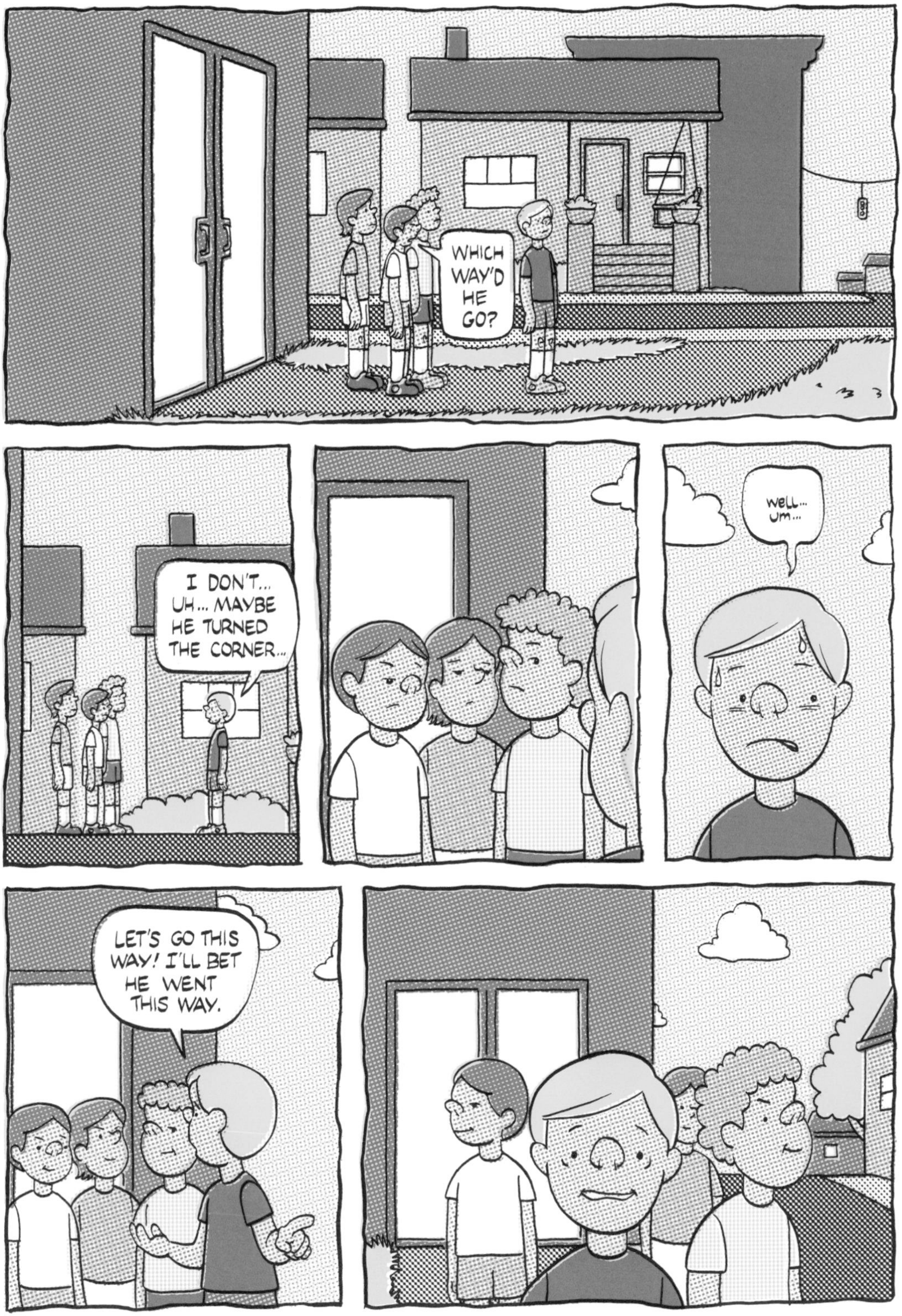
WHICH WAY'D HE GO?
I DON'T... UH... MAYBE HE TURNED THE CORNER...
well... um...
LET'S GO THIS WAY! I'LL BET HE WENT THIS WAY.

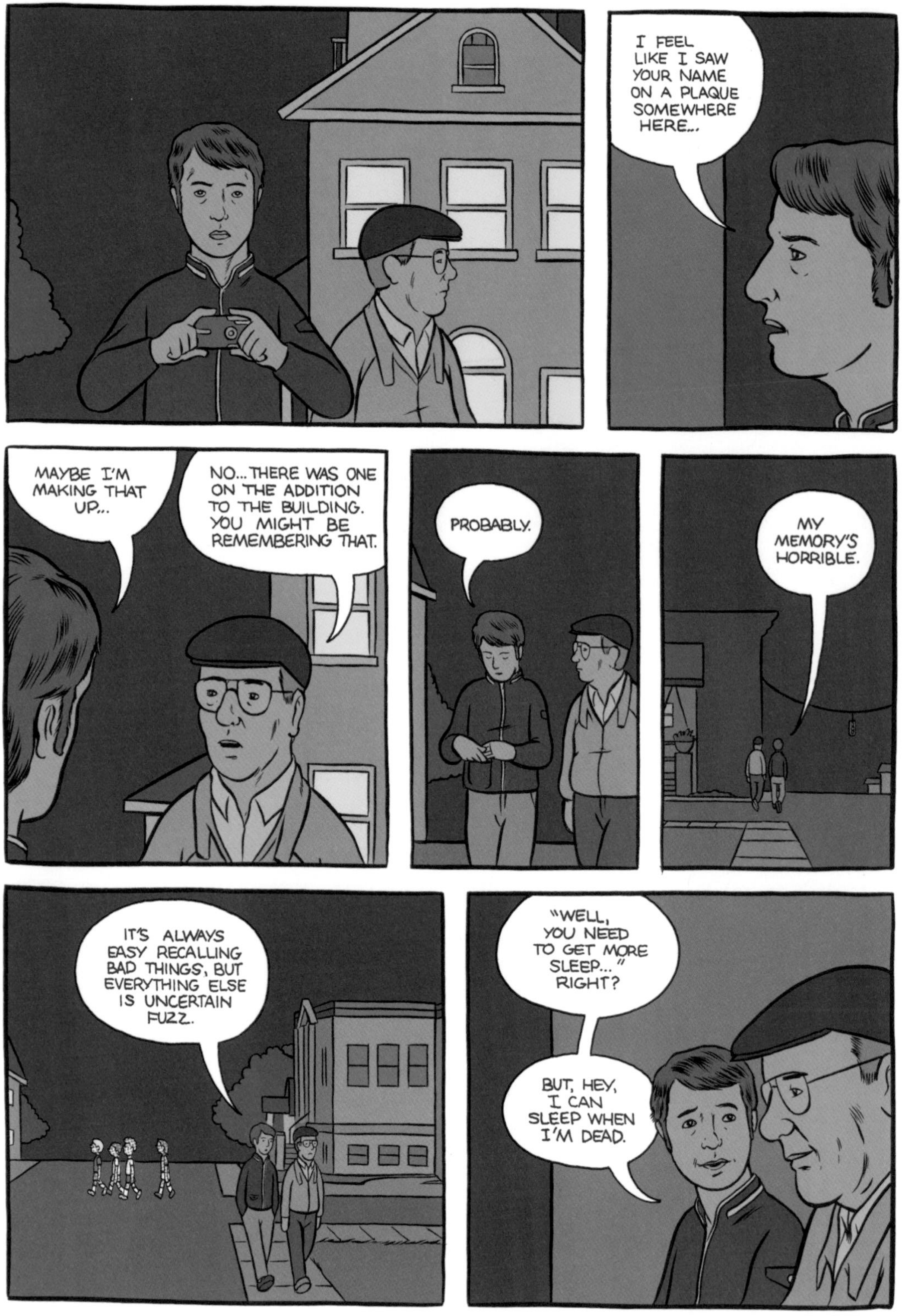
I FEEL LIKE I SAW YOUR NAME ON A PLAQUE SOMEWHERE HERE...
MAYBE I'M MAKING THAT UP...
NO... THERE WAS ONE ON THE ADDITION TO THE BUILDING. YOU MIGHT BE REMEMBERING THAT.
PROBABLY.
MY MEMORY'S HORRIBLE.
IT'S ALWAYS EASY RECALLING BAD THINGS, BUT EVERYTHING ELSE IS UNCERTAIN FUZZ.
"WELL, YOU NEED TO GET MORE SLEEP..." RIGHT?
BUT, HEY, I CAN SLEEP WHEN I'M DEAD.

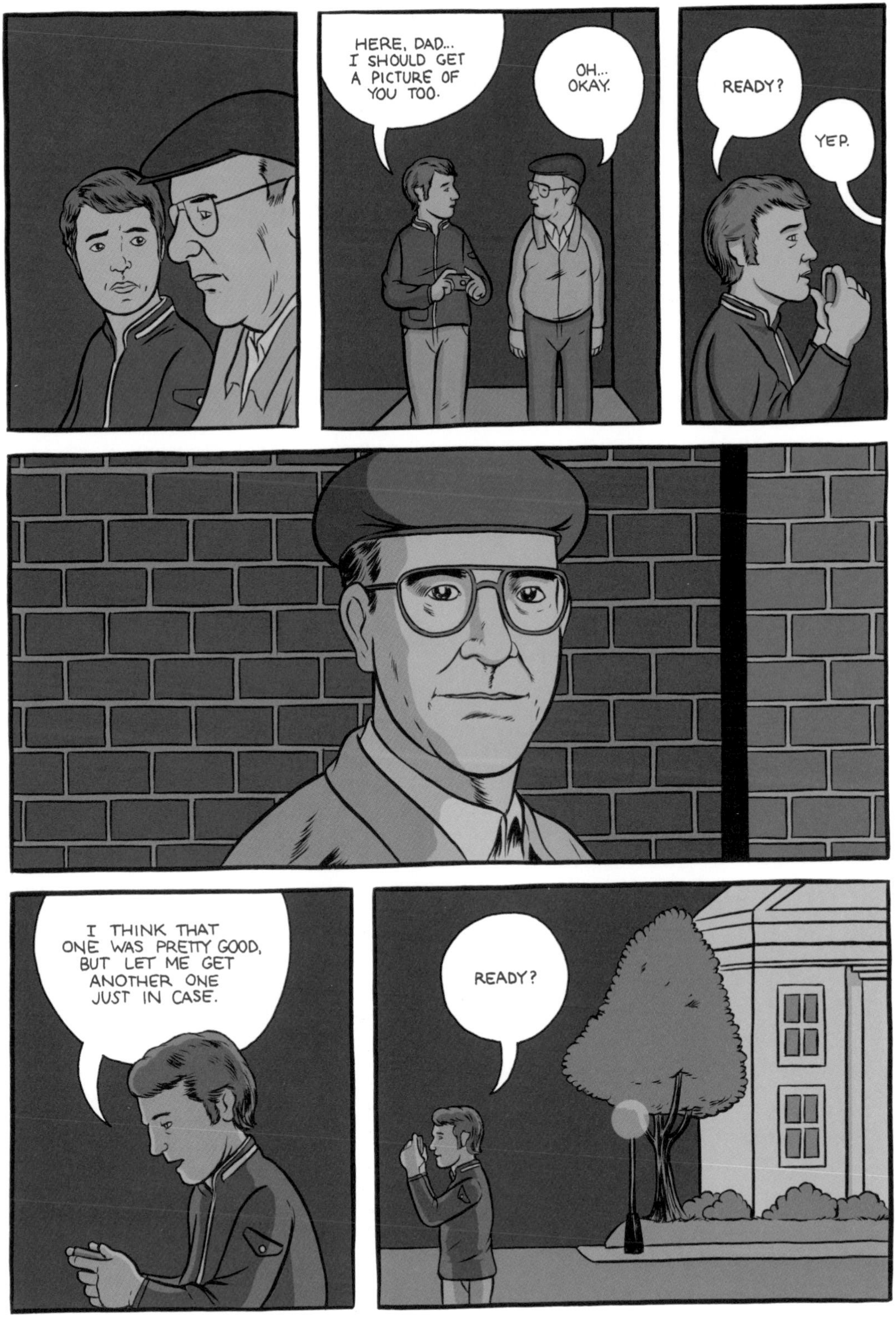
HERE, DAD... I SHOULD GET A PICTURE OF YOU TOO.
OH... OKAY.
READY?
YEP.
I THINK THAT ONE WAS PRETTY GOOD, BUT LET ME GET ANOTHER ONE JUST IN CASE.
READY?

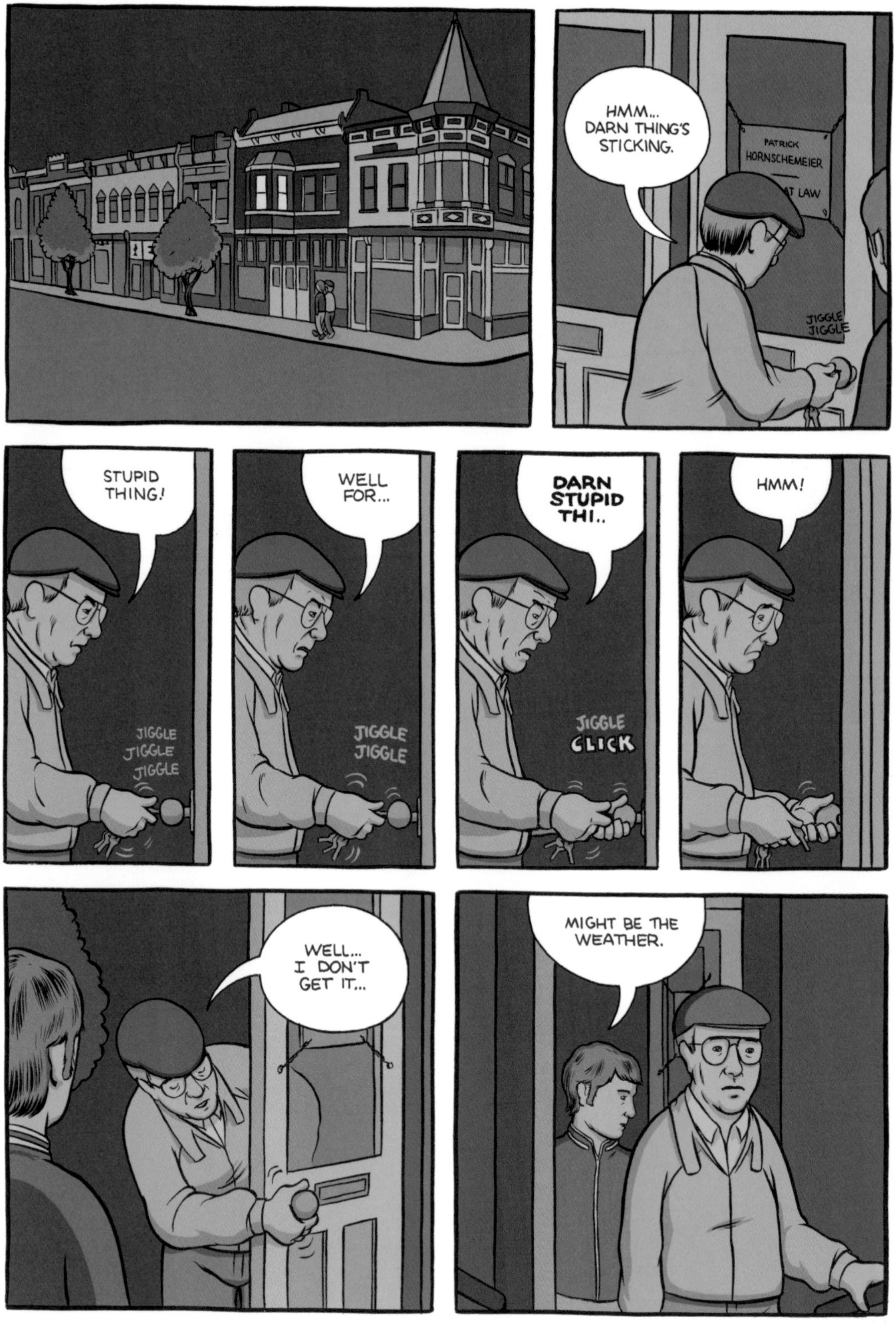
HMM... DARN THING'S STICKING.
PATRICK HORNSCHEMEIER
AT LAW
JIGGLE JIGGLE
STUPID THING!
JIGGLE JIGGLE JIGGLE
WELL FOR...
JIGGLE JIGGLE
DARN STUPID THI..
JIGGLE CLICK
HMM!
WELL... I DON'T GET IT...
MIGHT BE THE WEATHER.

DO YOU WANT ME TO LOCK THIS?
DOESN'T MATTER. WE WON'T BE HERE LONG.
YOU WANT ME TO JUST LEAVE IT UNLOCKED?
CLICK

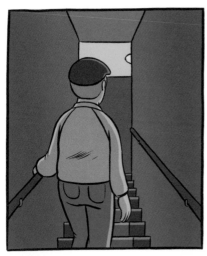

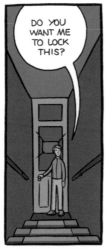

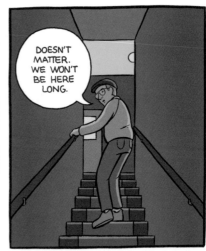

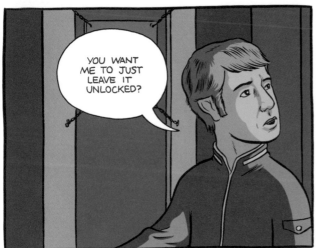

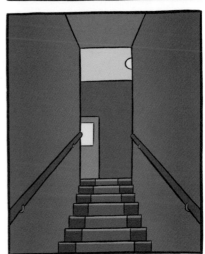

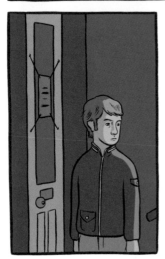

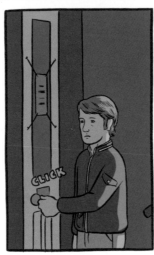

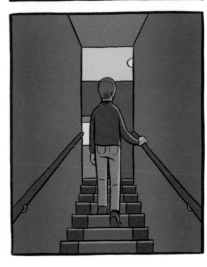

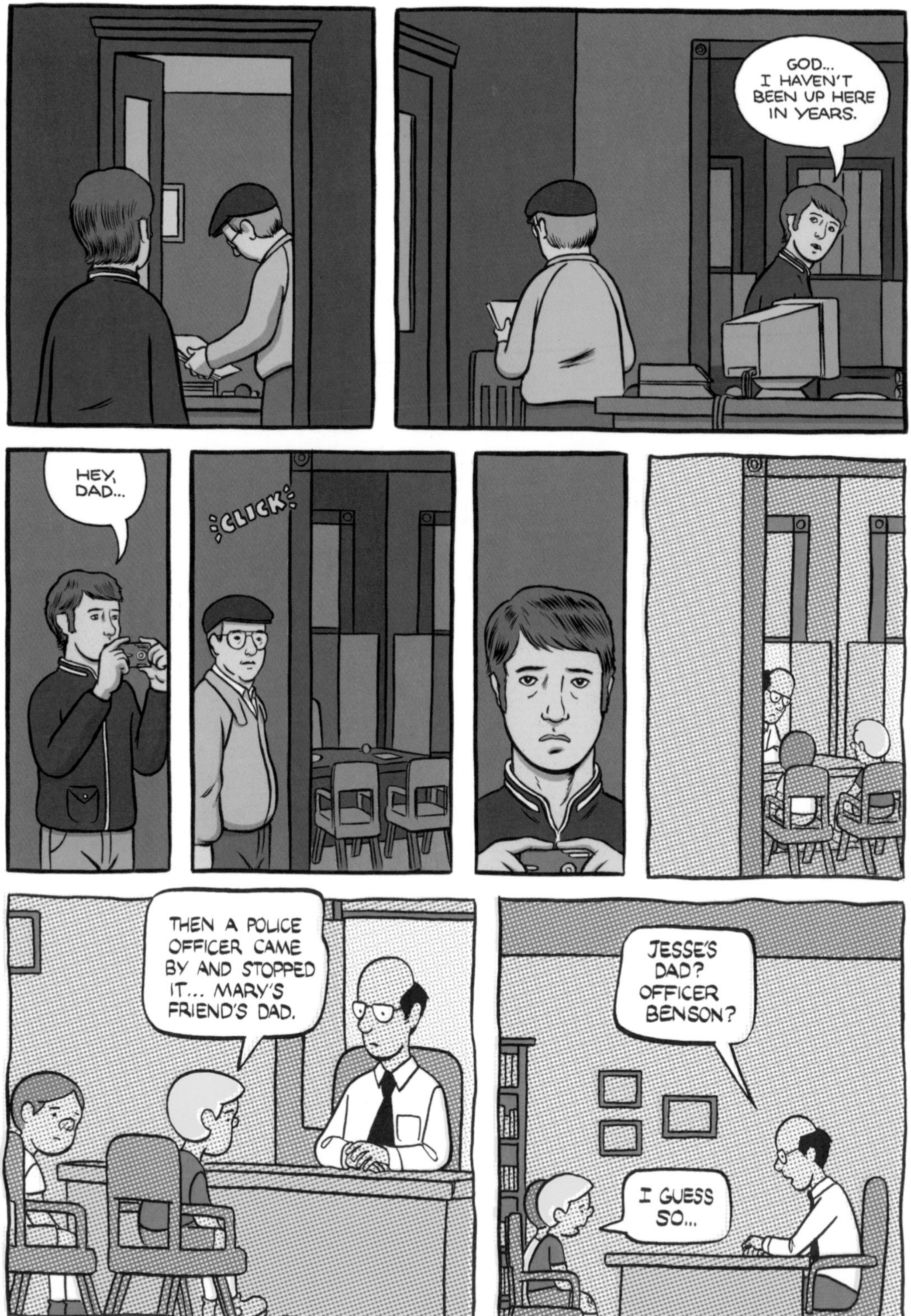
GOD... I HAVEN'T BEEN UP HERE IN YEARS.
HEY, DAD...
CLICK
THEN A POLICE OFFICER CAME BY AND STOPPED IT... MARY'S FRIEND'S DAD.
JESSE'S DAD? OFFICER BENSON?
I GUESS SO...

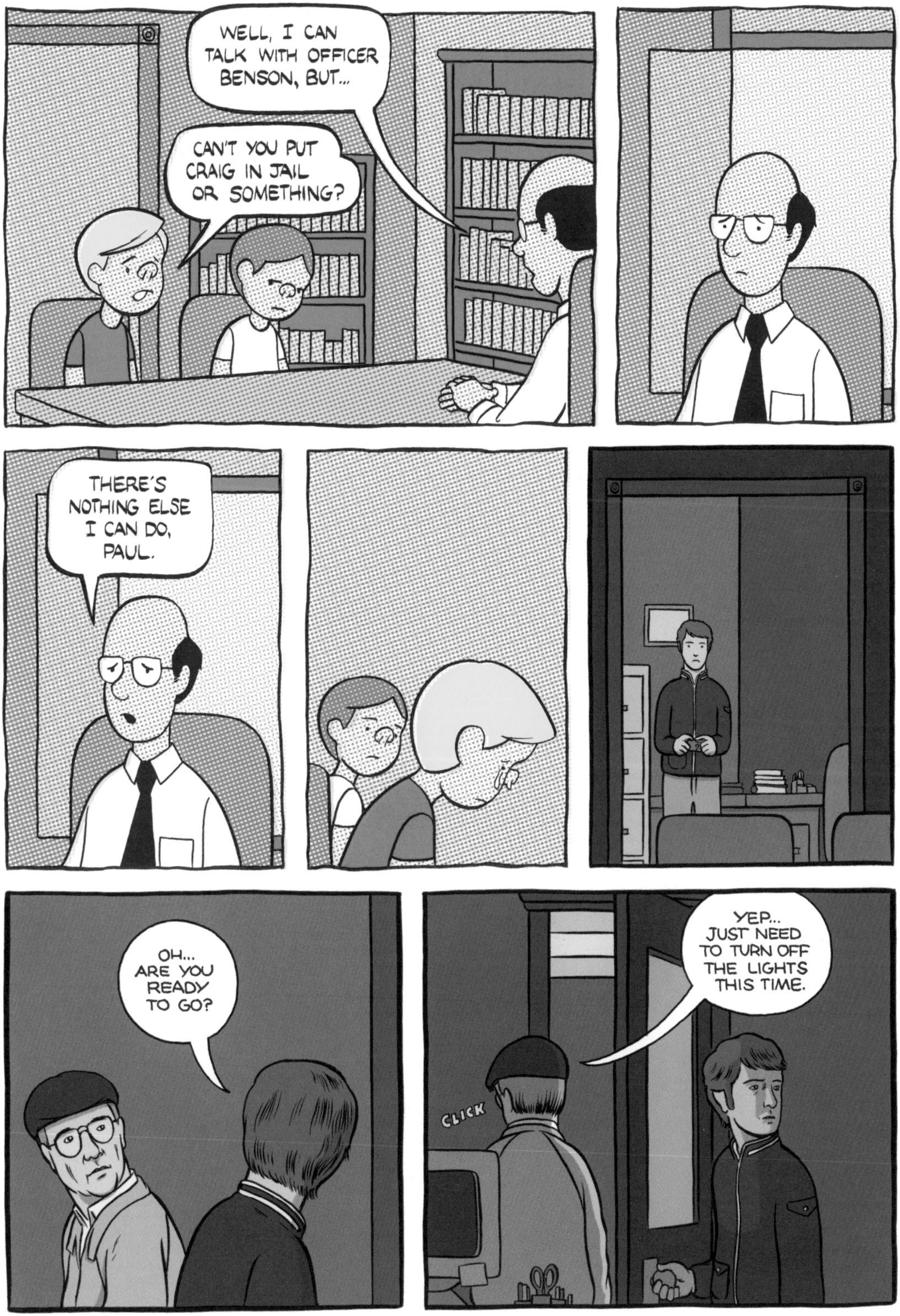
CAN'T YOU PUT CRAIG IN JAIL OR SOMETHING?
WELL, I CAN TALK WITH OFFICER BENSON, BUT...
THERE'S NOTHING ELSE I CAN DO, PAUL.
OH... ARE YOU READY TO GO?
YEP... JUST NEED TO TURN OFF THE LIGHTS THIS TIME.
CLICK

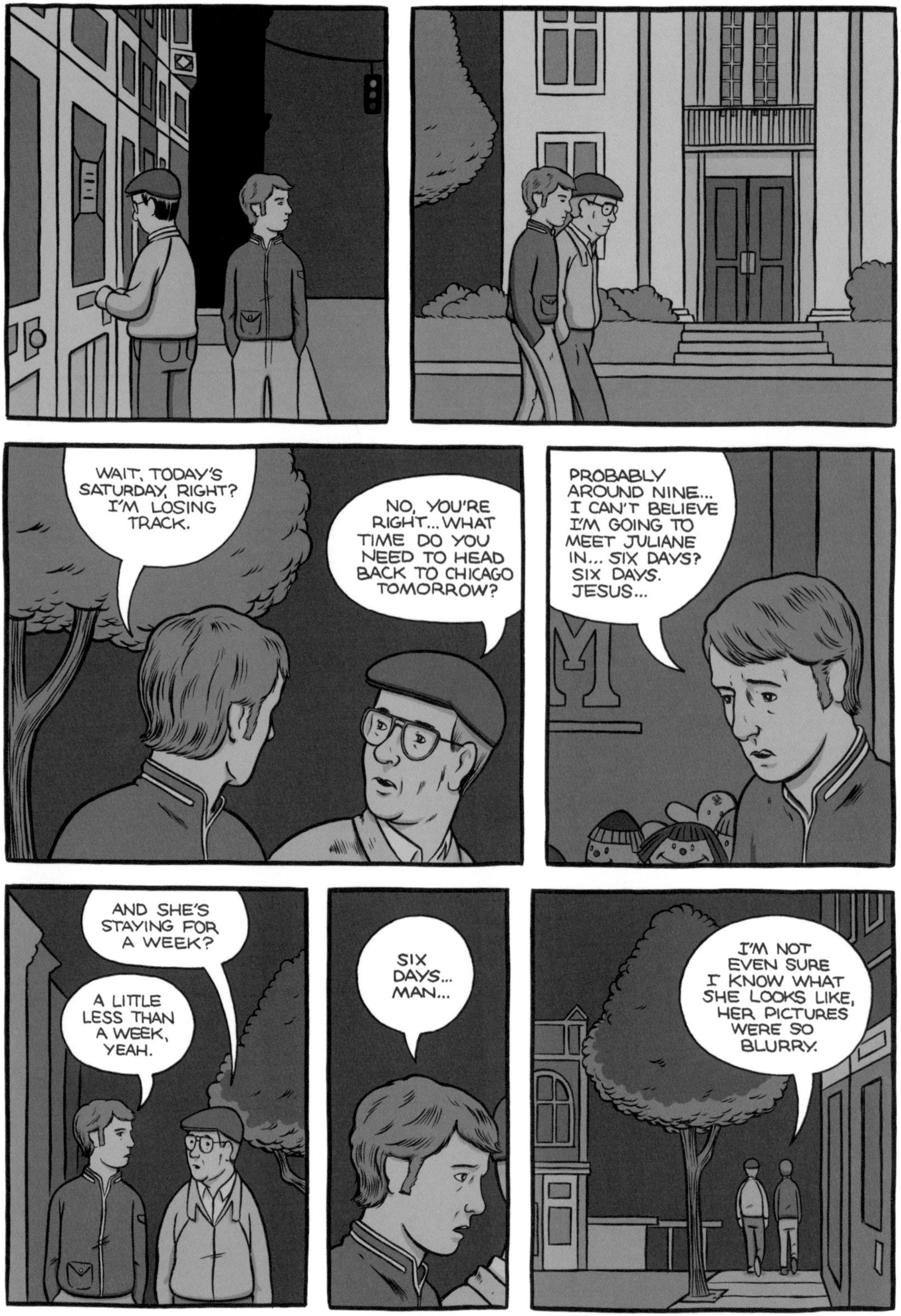
WAIT, TODAY'S SATURDAY, RIGHT? I'M LOSING TRACK.
NO, YOU'RE RIGHT... WHAT TIME DO YOU NEED TO HEAD BACK TO CHICAGO TOMORROW?
PROBABLY AROUND NINE... I CAN'T BELIEVE I'M GOING TO MEET JULIANE IN... SIX DAYS? SIX DAYS. JESUS...
AND SHE'S STAYING FOR A WEEK?
A LITTLE LESS THAN A WEEK, YEAH.
SIX DAYS... MAN...
I'M NOT EVEN SURE I KNOW WHAT SHE LOOKS LIKE, HER PICTURES WERE SO BLURRY.

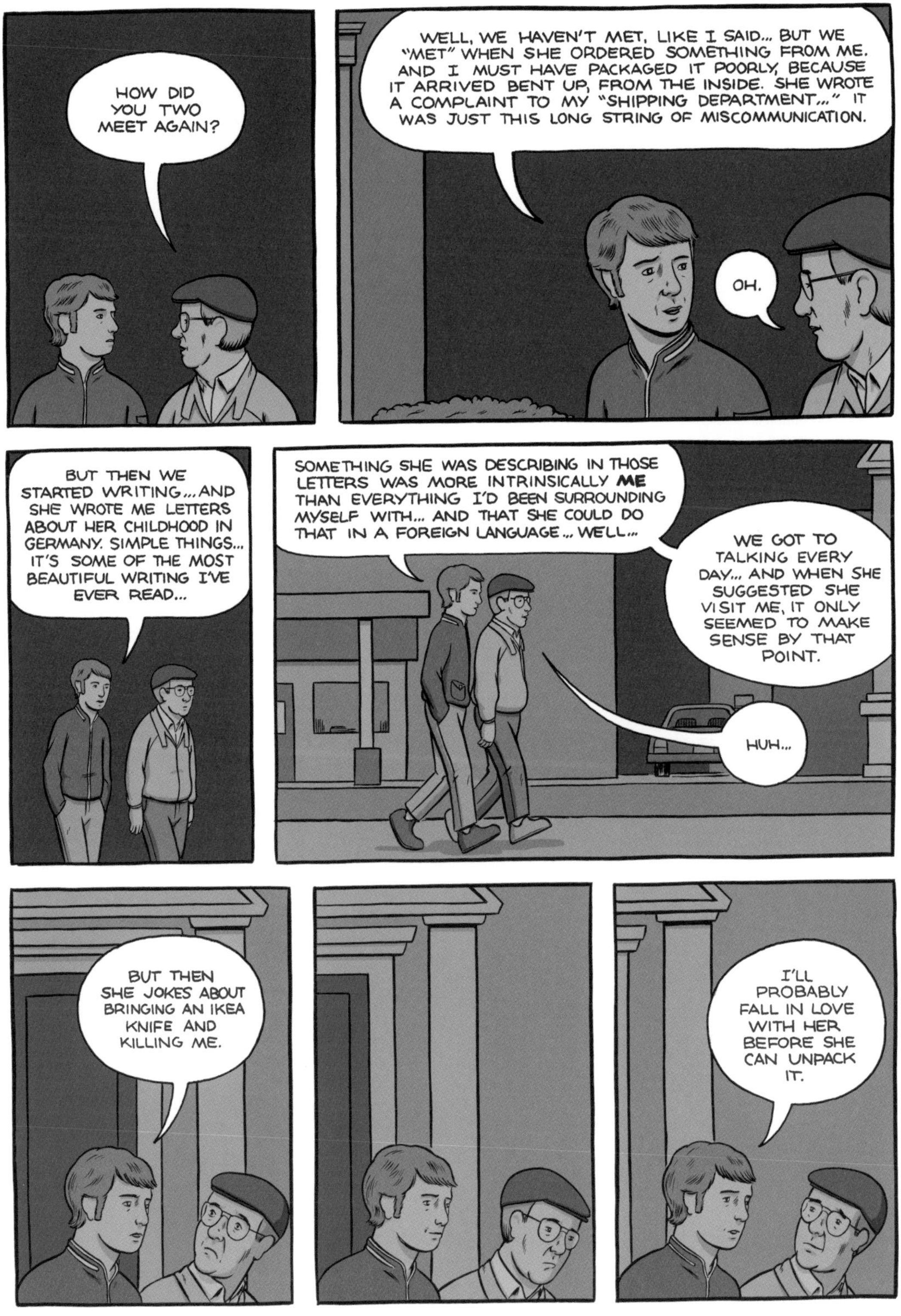
HOW DID YOU TWO MEET AGAIN?
WELL, WE HAVEN'T MET, LIKE I SAID... BUT WE "MET" WHEN SHE ORDERED SOMETHING FROM ME. AND I MUST HAVE PACKAGED IT POORLY, BECAUSE IT ARRIVED BENT UP, FROM THE INSIDE. SHE WROTE A COMPLAINT TO MY "SHIPPING DEPARTMENT..." IT WAS JUST THIS LONG STRING OF MISCOMMUNICATION.
OH.
BUT THEN WE STARTED WRITING... AND SHE WROTE ME LETTERS ABOUT HER CHILDHOOD IN GERMANY. SIMPLE THINGS... IT'S SOME OF THE MOST BEAUTIFUL WRITING I'VE EVER READ...
SOMETHING SHE WAS DESCRIBING IN THOSE LETTERS WAS MORE INTRINSICALLY **ME** THAN EVERYTHING I'D BEEN SURROUNDING MYSELF WITH... AND THAT SHE COULD DO THAT IN A FOREIGN LANGUAGE... WELL...
WE GOT TO TALKING EVERY DAY... AND WHEN SHE SUGGESTED SHE VISIT ME, IT ONLY SEEMED TO MAKE SENSE BY THAT POINT.
HUH...
BUT THEN SHE JOKES ABOUT BRINGING AN IKEA KNIFE AND KILLING ME.
I'LL PROBABLY FALL IN LOVE WITH HER BEFORE SHE CAN UNPACK IT.

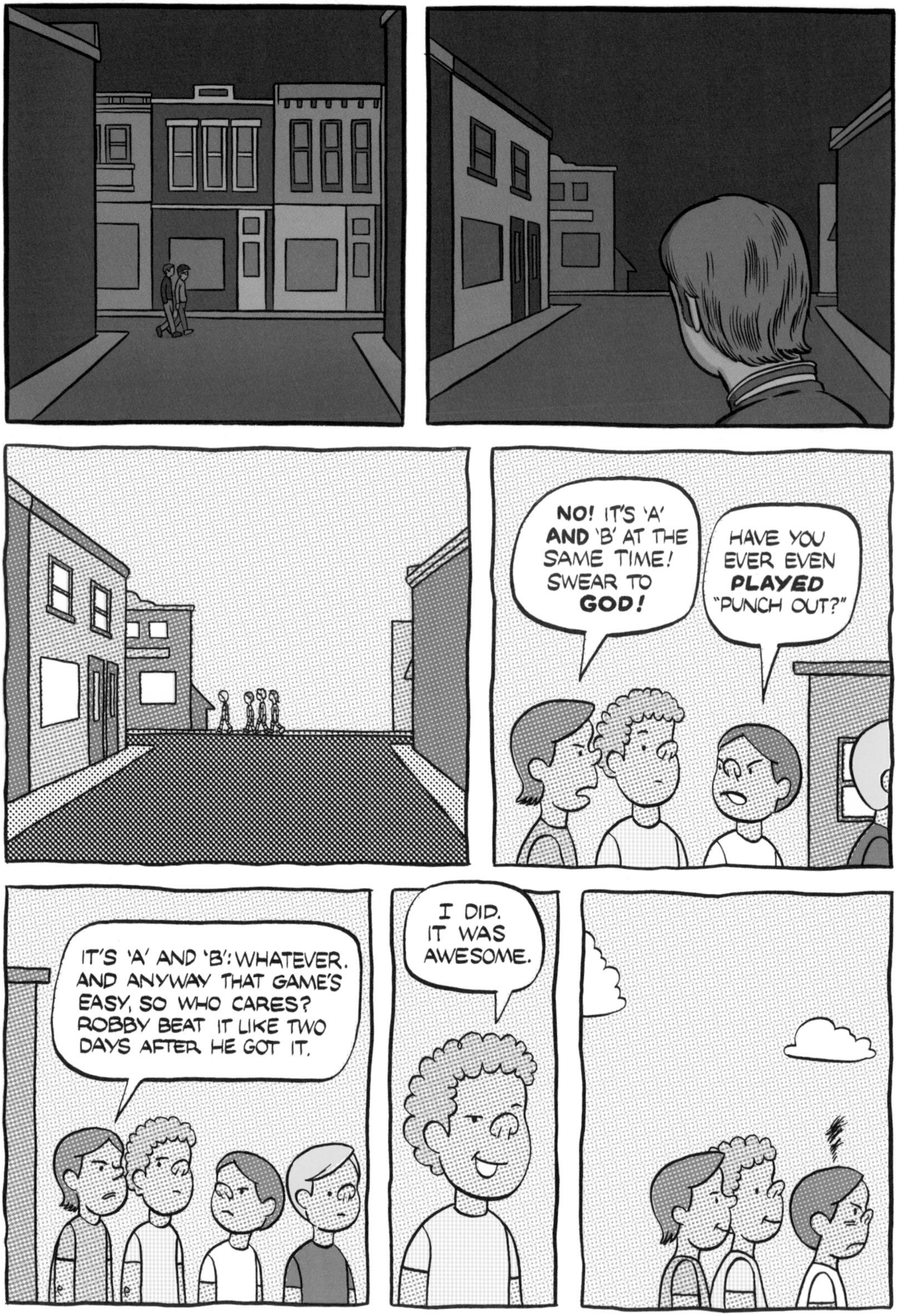
NO! IT'S 'A' AND 'B' AT THE SAME TIME! SWEAR TO GOD!
HAVE YOU EVER EVEN PLAYED "PUNCH OUT?"
IT'S 'A' AND 'B': WHATEVER. AND ANYWAY THAT GAME'S EASY, SO WHO CARES? ROBBY BEAT IT LIKE TWO DAYS AFTER HE GOT IT.
I DID. IT WAS AWESOME.

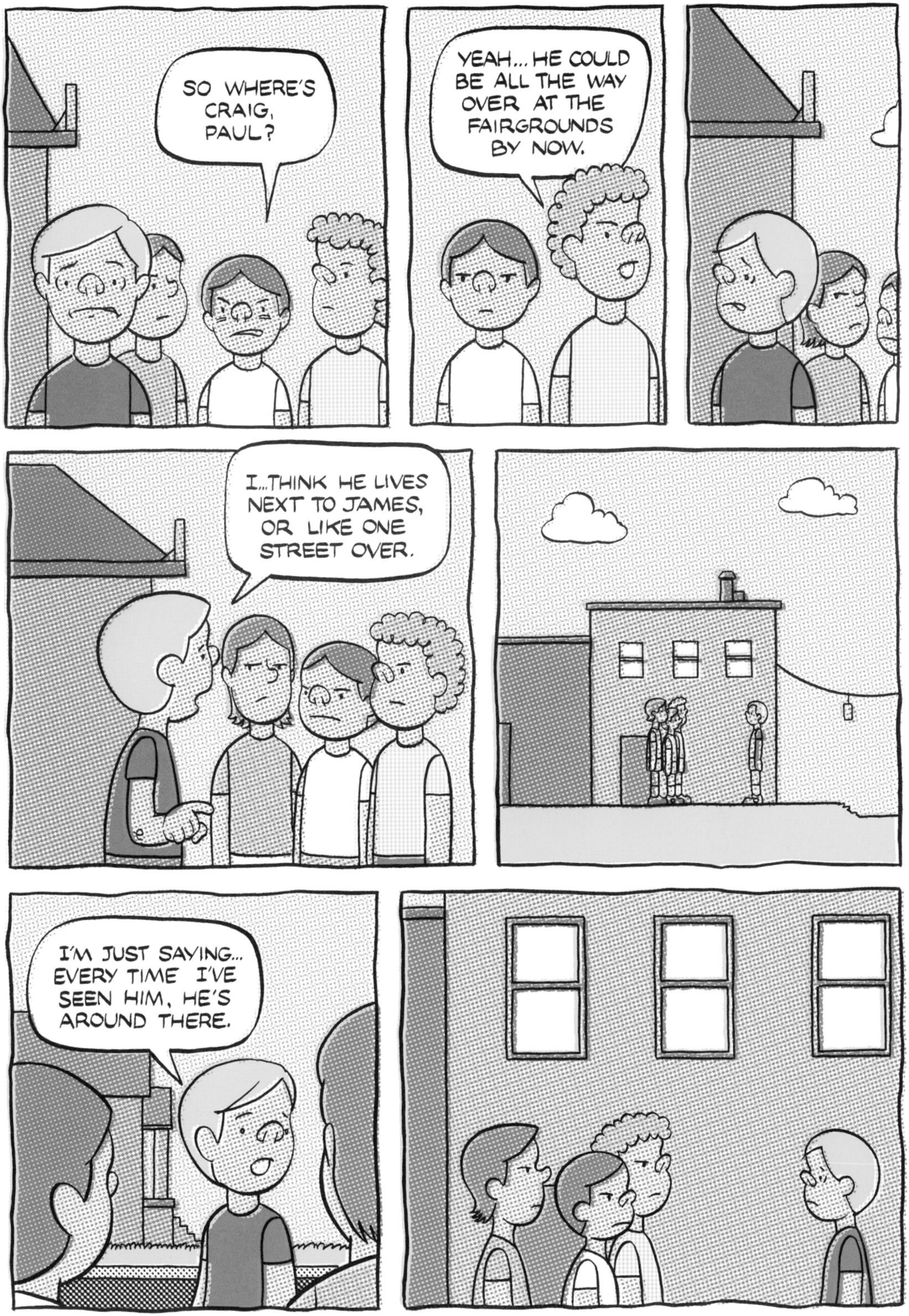
SO WHERE'S CRAIG, PAUL?
YEAH... HE COULD BE ALL THE WAY OVER AT THE FAIRGROUNDS BY NOW.
I...THINK HE LIVES NEXT TO JAMES, OR LIKE ONE STREET OVER.
I'M JUST SAYING... EVERY TIME I'VE SEEN HIM, HE'S AROUND THERE.

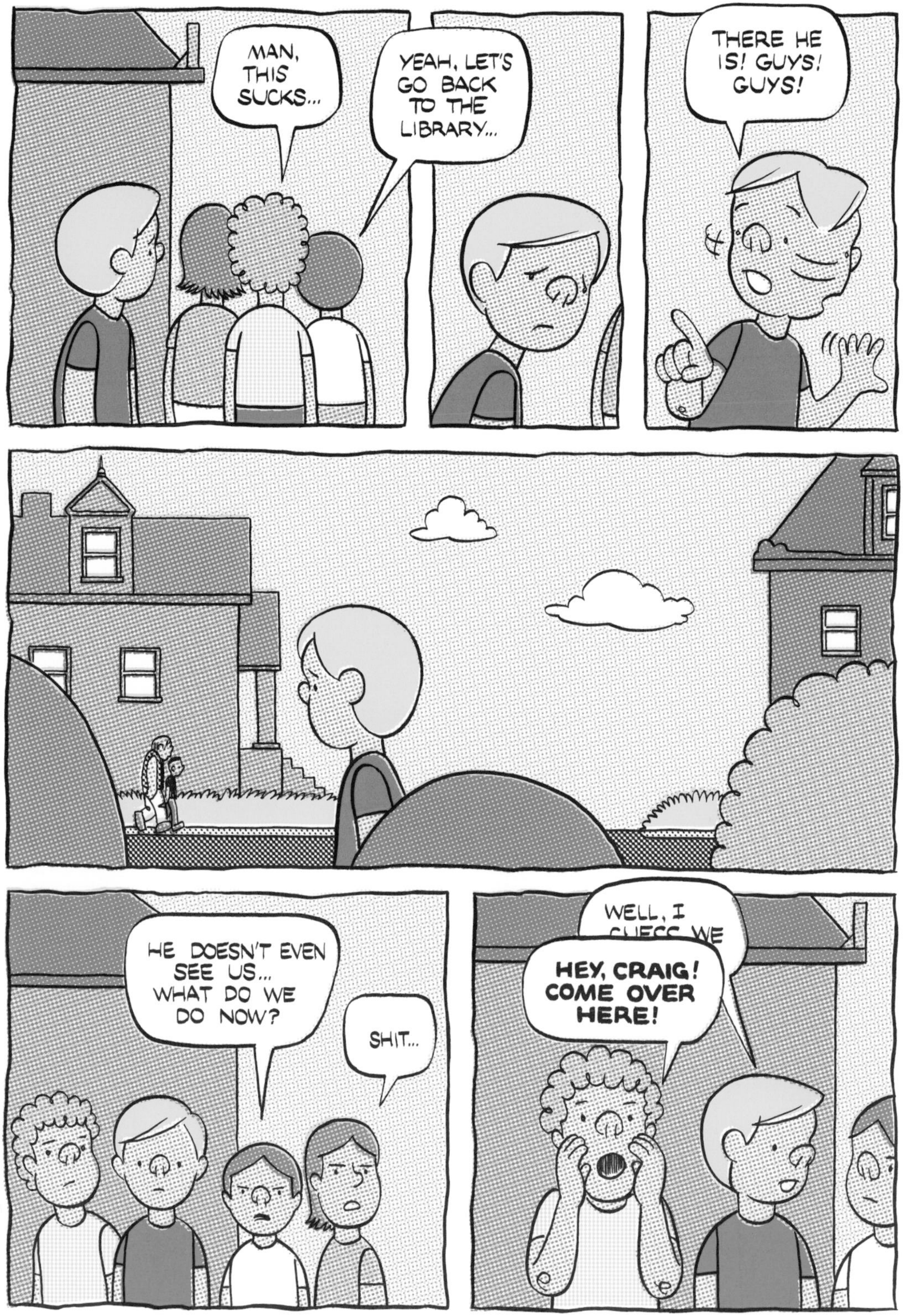
MAN, THIS SUCKS...
YEAH, LET'S GO BACK TO THE LIBRARY...
THERE HE IS! GUYS! GUYS!
HE DOESN'T EVEN SEE US... WHAT DO WE DO NOW?
SHIT...
WELL, I
HEY, CRAIG! COME OVER HERE!

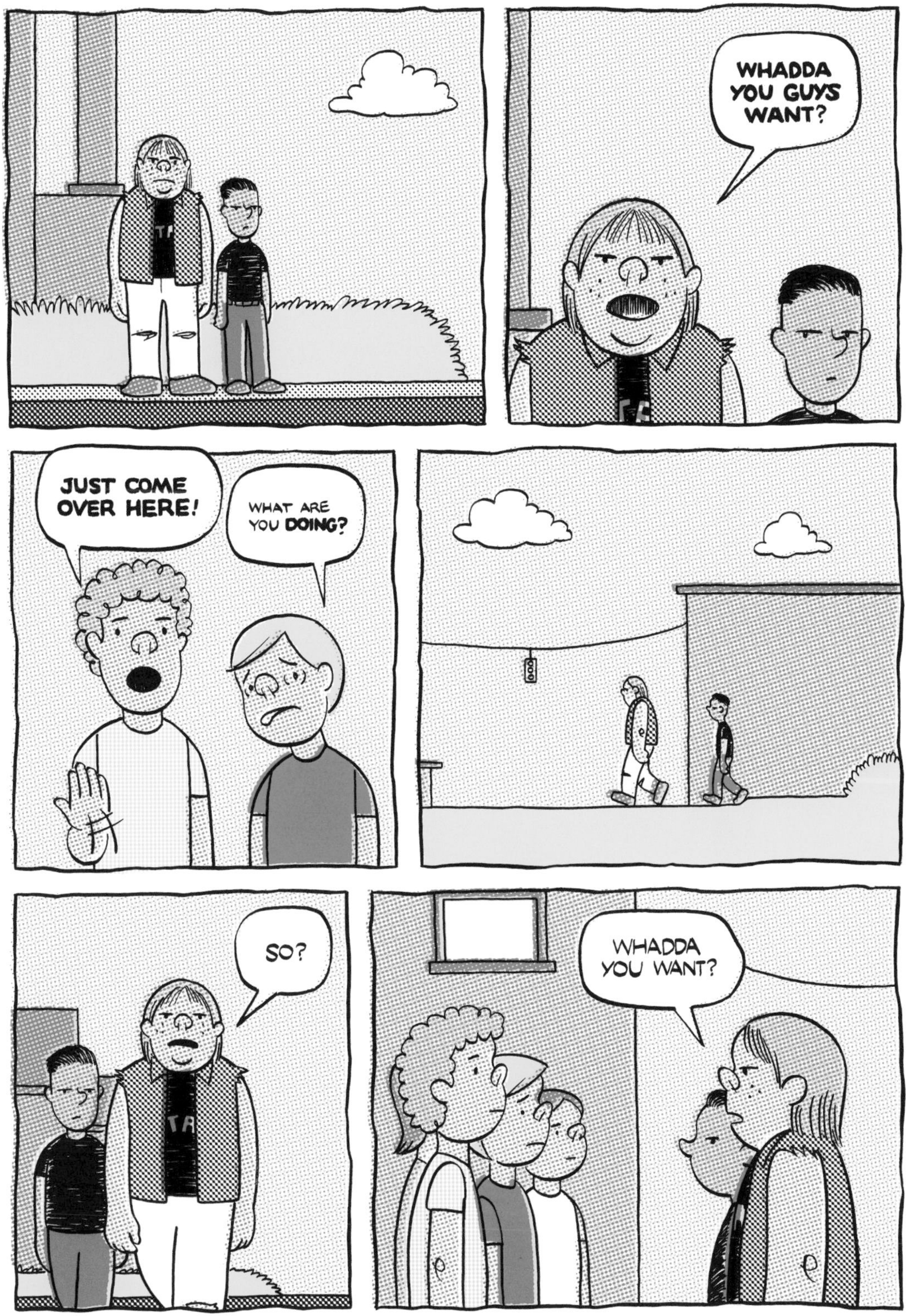
WHADDA YOU GUYS WANT?
JUST COME OVER HERE!
WHAT ARE YOU DOING?
SO?
WHADDA YOU WANT?

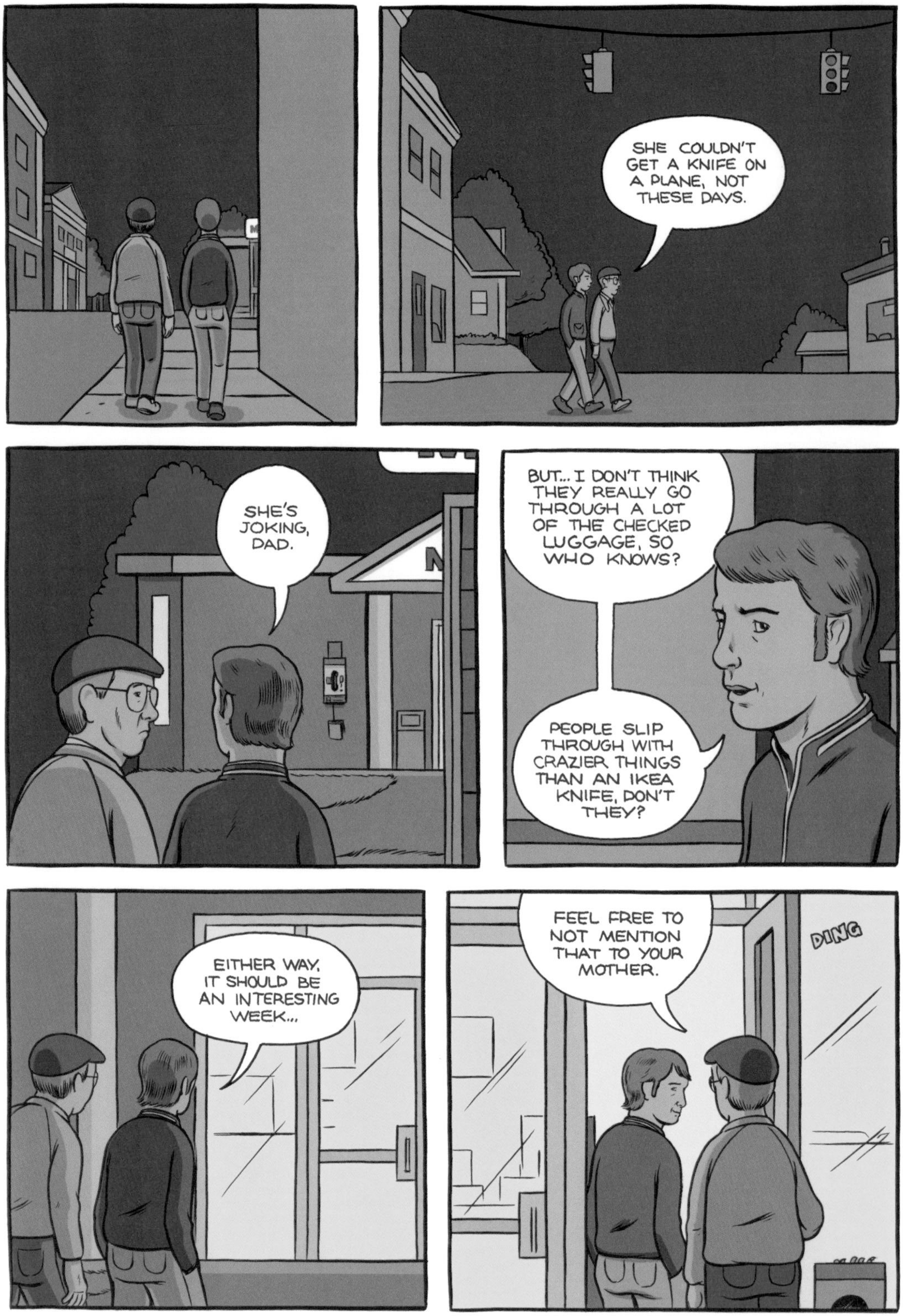
SHE COULDN'T GET A KNIFE ON A PLANE, NOT THESE DAYS.
SHE'S JOKING, DAD.
BUT... I DON'T THINK THEY REALLY GO THROUGH A LOT OF THE CHECKED LUGGAGE, SO WHO KNOWS?
PEOPLE SLIP THROUGH WITH CRAZIER THINGS THAN AN IKEA KNIFE, DON'T THEY?
EITHER WAY, IT SHOULD BE AN INTERESTING WEEK...
FEEL FREE TO NOT MENTION THAT TO YOUR MOTHER.
DING

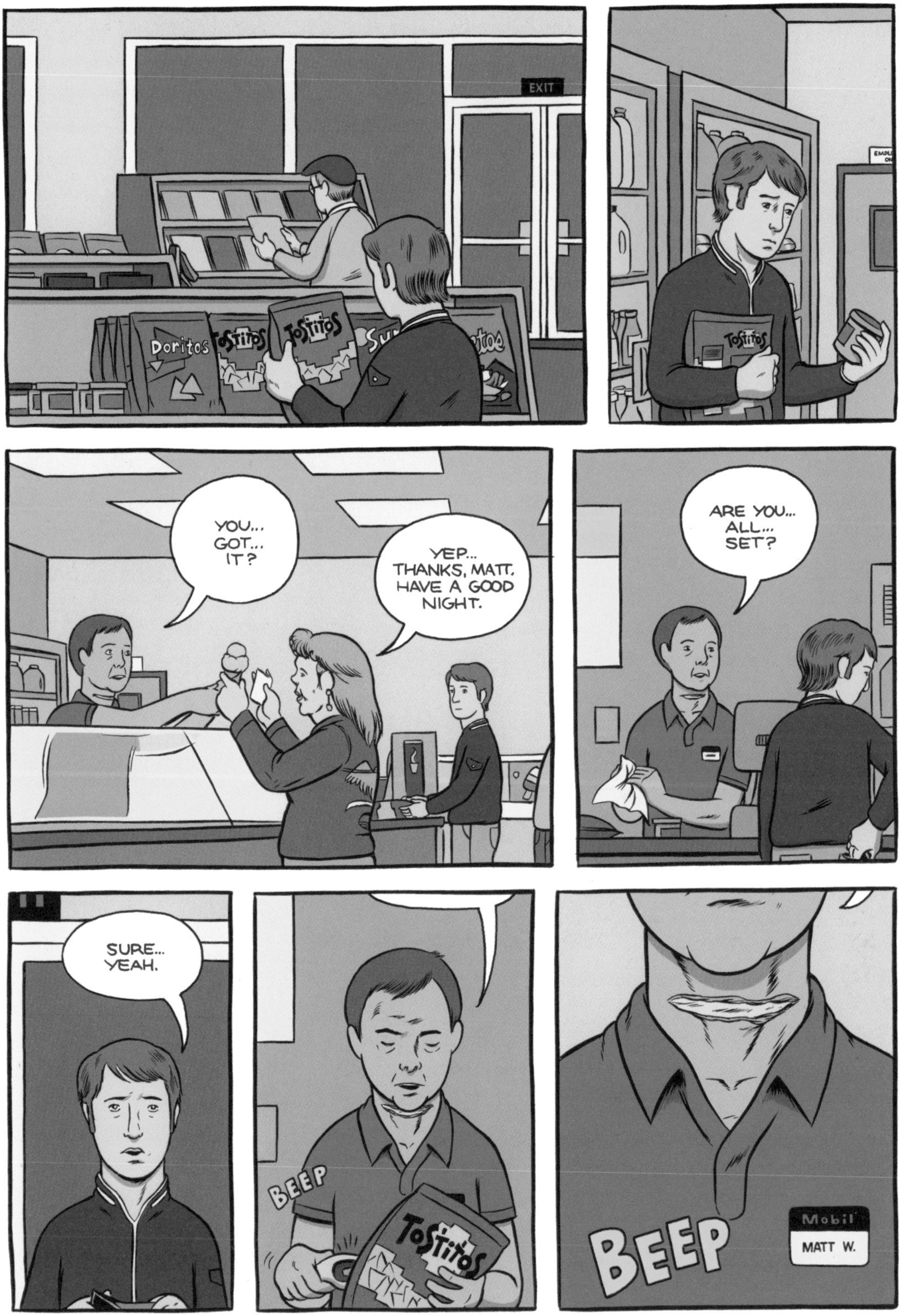
EXIT
Doritos
TOSTITOS
TOSTITOS
YOU... GOT... IT?
YEP... THANKS, MATT. HAVE A GOOD NIGHT.
ARE YOU... ALL... SET?
SURE... YEAH.
BEEP
TOSTITOS
BEEP
Mobil
MATT W.

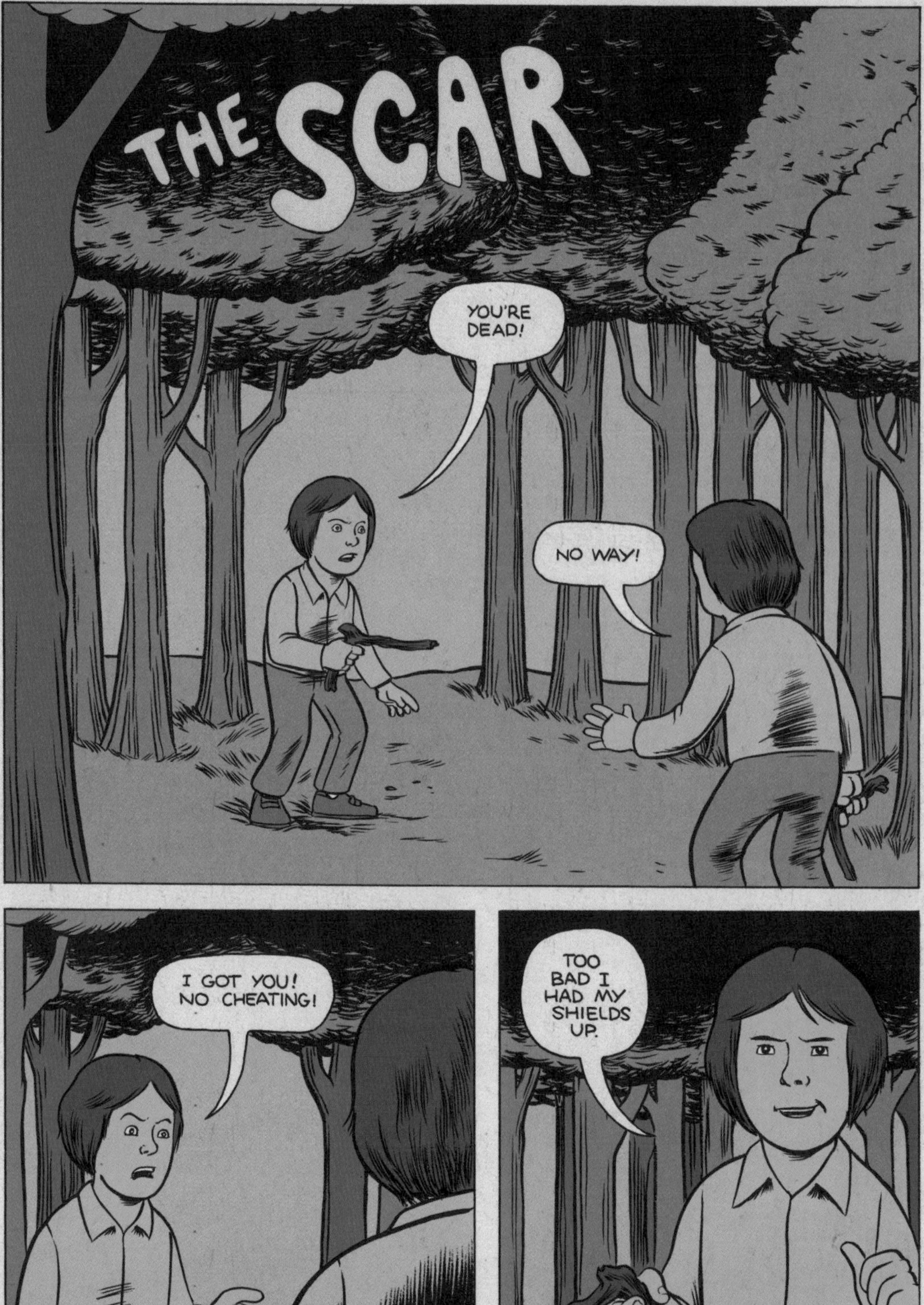
THE SCAR
YOU'RE DEAD!
NO WAY!
I GOT YOU! NO CHEATING!
TOO BAD I HAD MY SHIELDS UP.

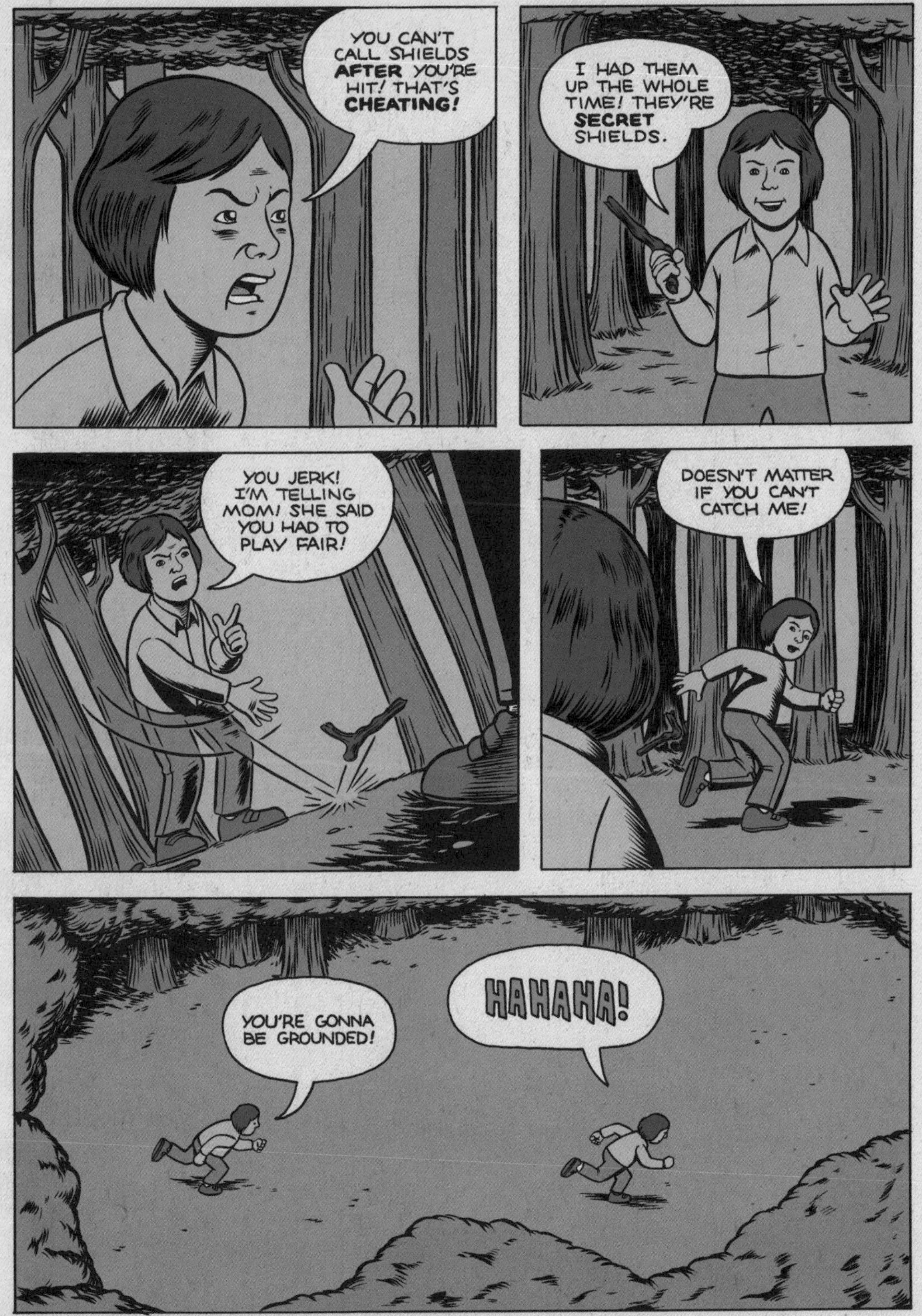
YOU CAN'T CALL SHIELDS **AFTER** YOU'RE HIT! THAT'S **CHEATING!**
I HAD THEM UP THE WHOLE TIME! THEY'RE **SECRET** SHIELDS.
YOU JERK! I'M TELLING MOM! SHE SAID YOU HAD TO PLAY FAIR!
DOESN'T MATTER IF YOU CAN'T CATCH ME!
YOU'RE GONNA BE GROUNDED!
HAHAHA!

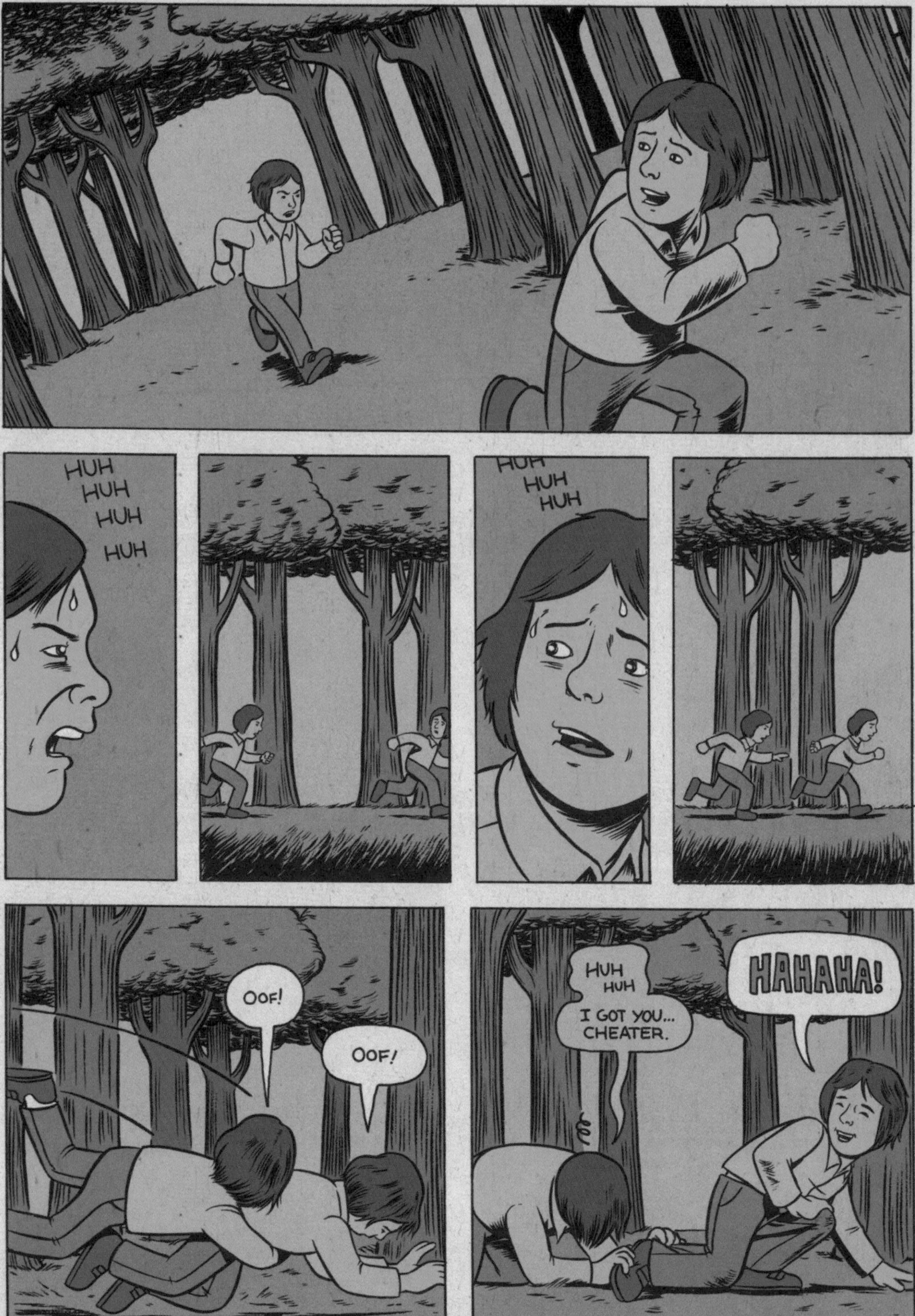
HUH
HUH
HUH
HUH
HUH
HUH
HUH
OOF!
OOF!
HUH HUH
I GOT YOU... CHEATER.
HAHAHA!

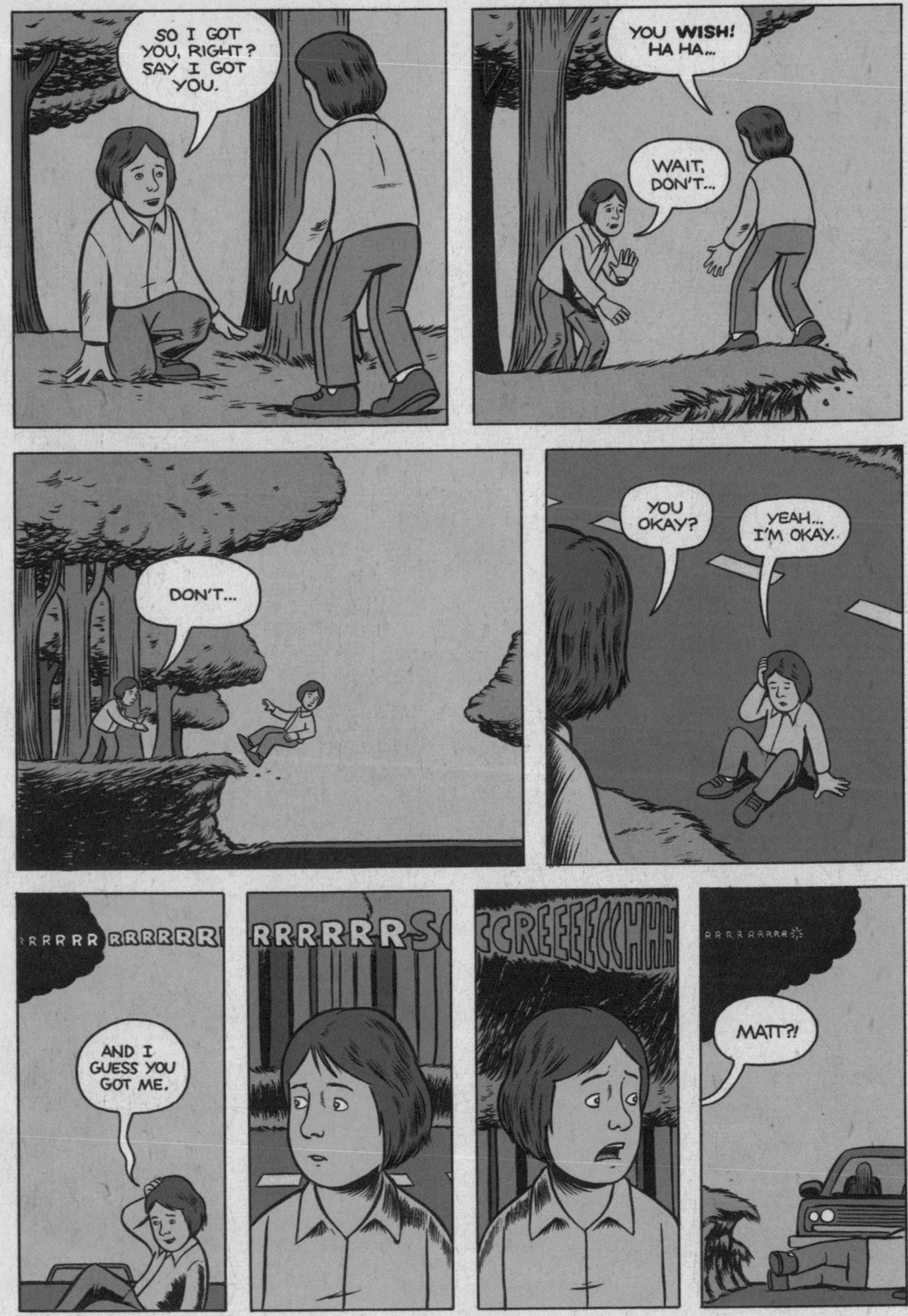
SO I GOT YOU, RIGHT? SAY I GOT YOU.
YOU **WISH!** HA HA...
WAIT, DON'T...
DON'T...
YOU OKAY?
YEAH... I'M OKAY.
RRRRRR RRRRRRR
AND I GUESS YOU GOT ME.
RRRRRRS
CCREEEECCHHH
RRRRRRRRR
MATT?!

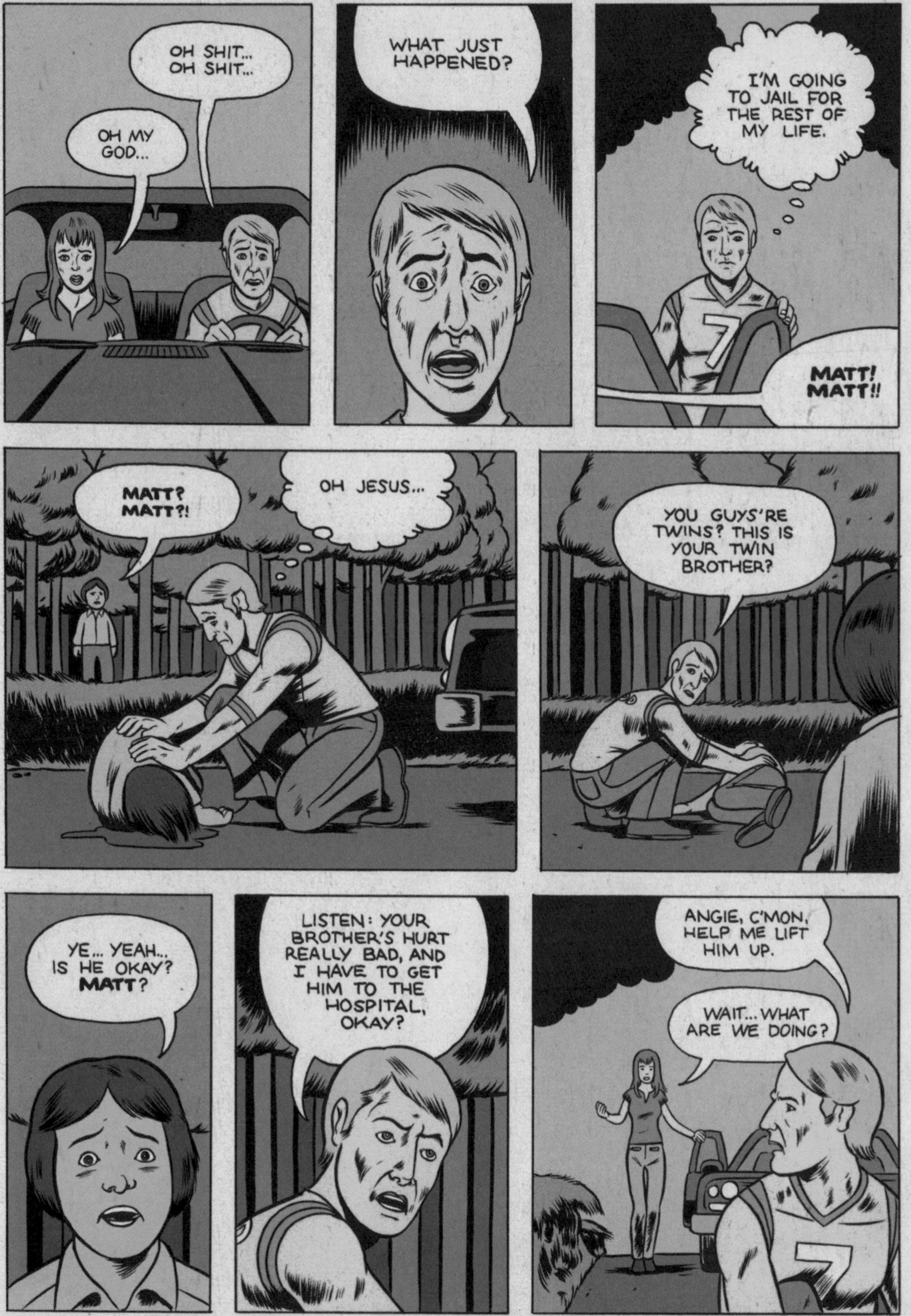
OH SHIT... OH SHIT...
OH MY GOD...
WHAT JUST HAPPENED?
I'M GOING TO JAIL FOR THE REST OF MY LIFE.
MATT! MATT!!
MATT? MATT?!
OH JESUS...
YOU GUYS'RE TWINS? THIS IS YOUR TWIN BROTHER?
YE... YEAH... IS HE OKAY? MATT?
LISTEN: YOUR BROTHER'S HURT REALLY BAD, AND I HAVE TO GET HIM TO THE HOSPITAL, OKAY?
ANGIE, C'MON, HELP ME LIFT HIM UP.
WAIT... WHAT ARE WE DOING?

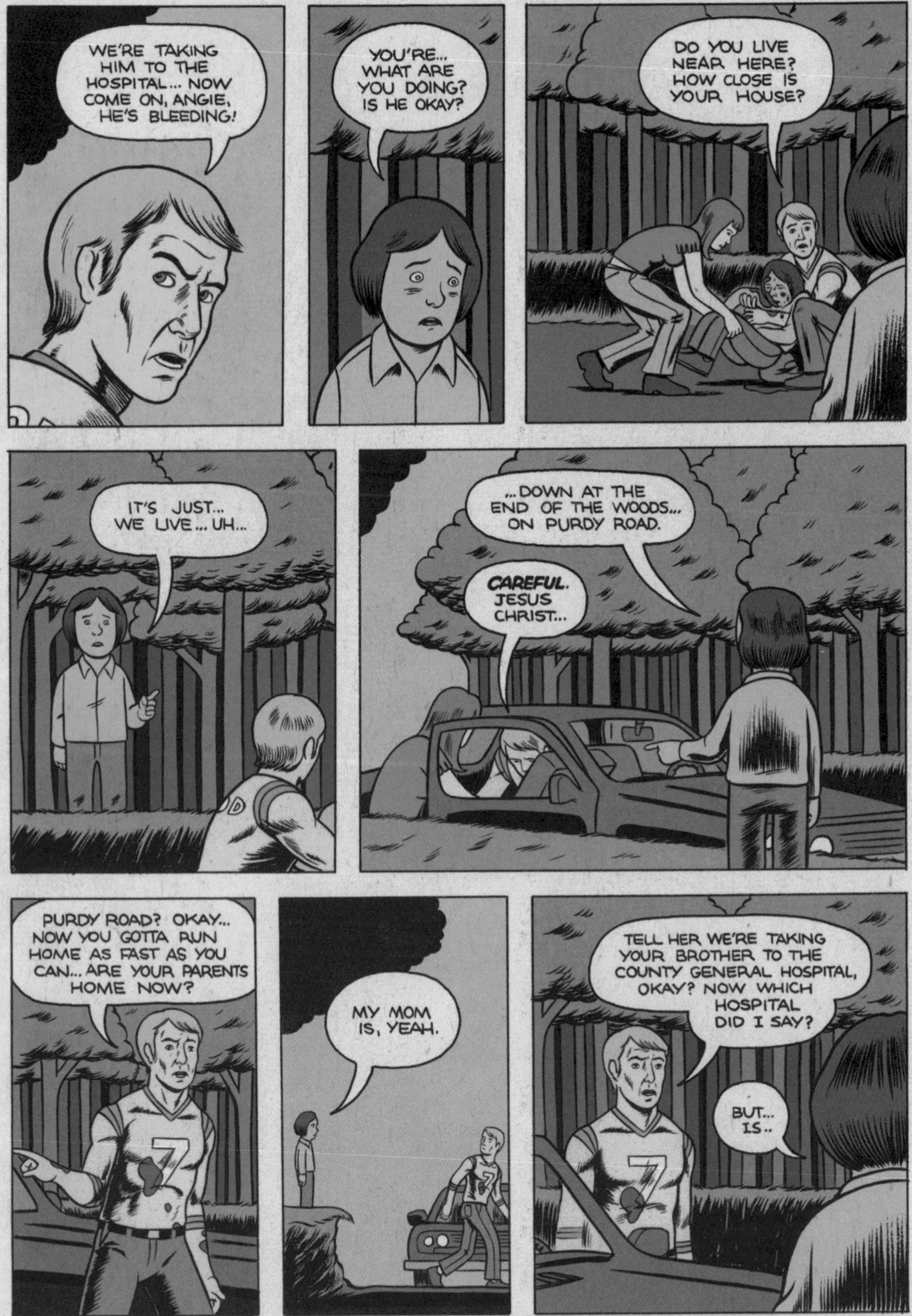
WE'RE TAKING HIM TO THE HOSPITAL... NOW COME ON, ANGIE, HE'S BLEEDING!
YOU'RE... WHAT ARE YOU DOING? IS HE OKAY?
DO YOU LIVE NEAR HERE? HOW CLOSE IS YOUR HOUSE?
IT'S JUST... WE LIVE... UH...
...DOWN AT THE END OF THE WOODS... ON PURDY ROAD.
CAREFUL. JESUS CHRIST...
PURDY ROAD? OKAY... NOW YOU GOTTA RUN HOME AS FAST AS YOU CAN... ARE YOUR PARENTS HOME NOW?
MY MOM IS, YEAH.
TELL HER WE'RE TAKING YOUR BROTHER TO THE COUNTY GENERAL HOSPITAL, OKAY? NOW WHICH HOSPITAL DID I SAY?
BUT... IS..

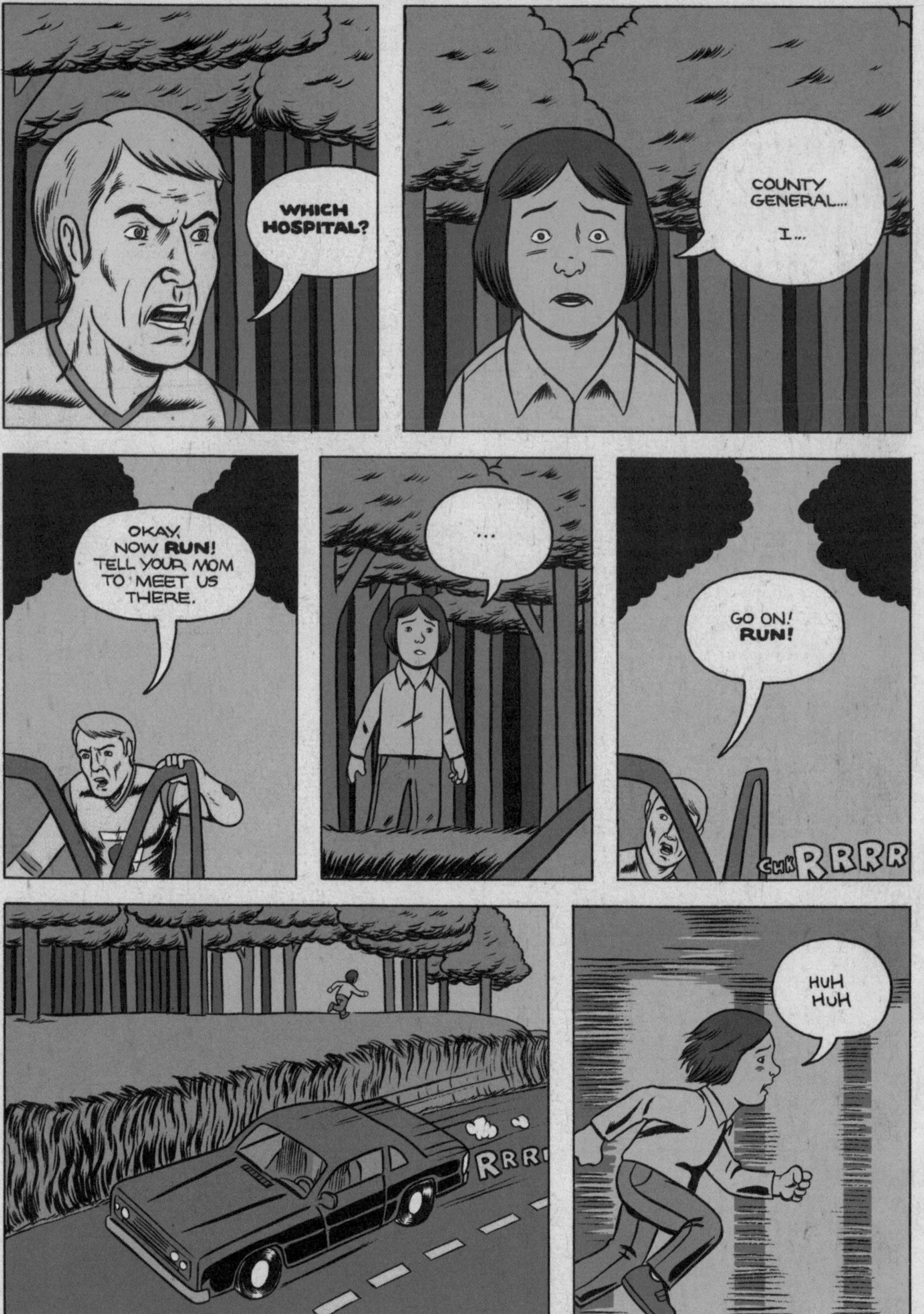

WHICH HOSPITAL?
COUNTY GENERAL... I...
OKAY, NOW RUN! TELL YOUR MOM TO MEET US THERE.
...
GO ON! RUN!
CHKRRRR
RRR
HUH HUH

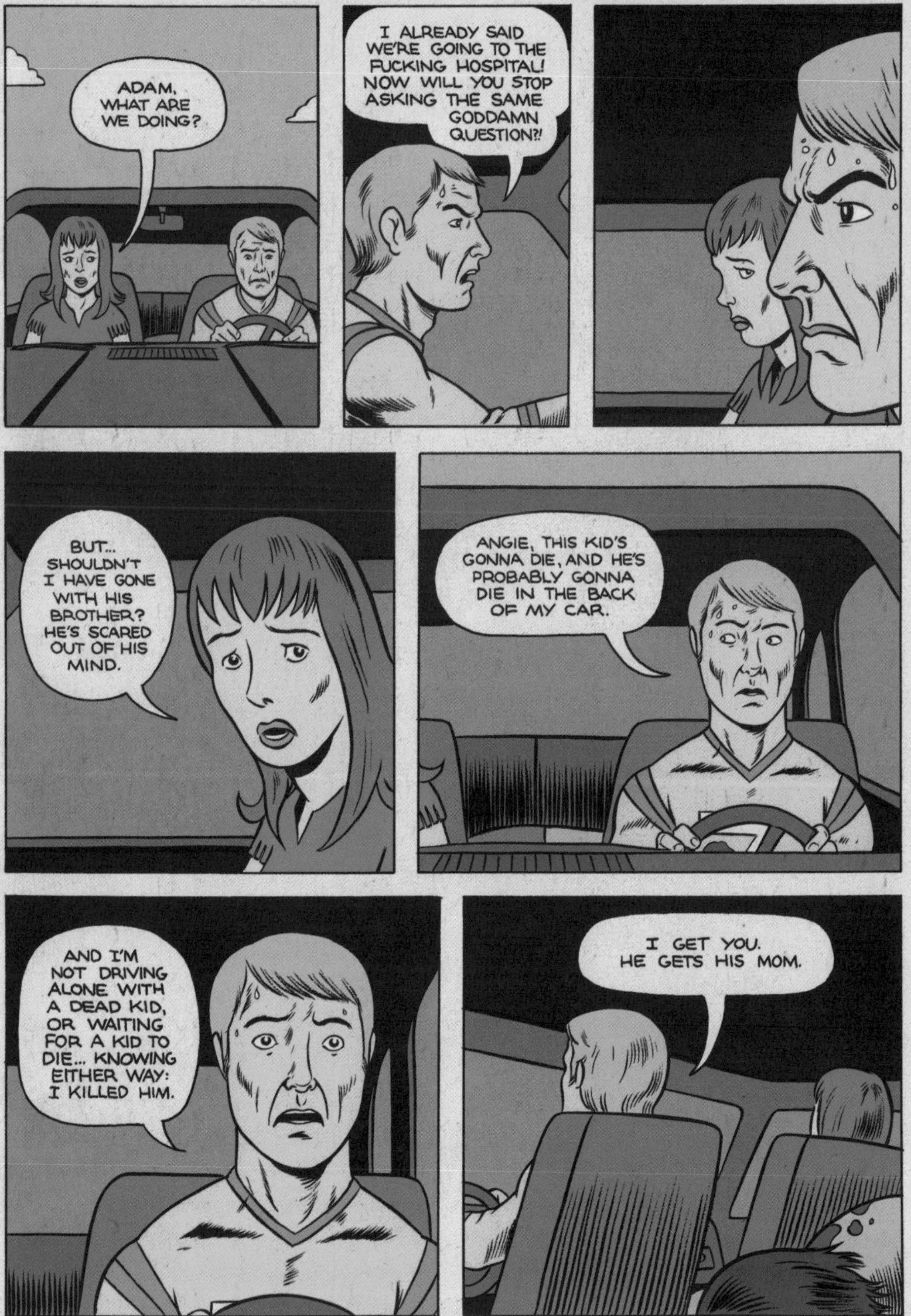
ADAM, WHAT ARE WE DOING?
I ALREADY SAID WE'RE GOING TO THE FUCKING HOSPITAL! NOW WILL YOU STOP ASKING THE SAME GODDAMN QUESTION?!
BUT... SHOULDN'T I HAVE GONE WITH HIS BROTHER? HE'S SCARED OUT OF HIS MIND.
ANGIE, THIS KID'S GONNA DIE, AND HE'S PROBABLY GONNA DIE IN THE BACK OF MY CAR.
AND I'M NOT DRIVING ALONE WITH A DEAD KID, OR WAITING FOR A KID TO DIE... KNOWING EITHER WAY: I KILLED HIM.
I GET YOU. HE GETS HIS MOM.

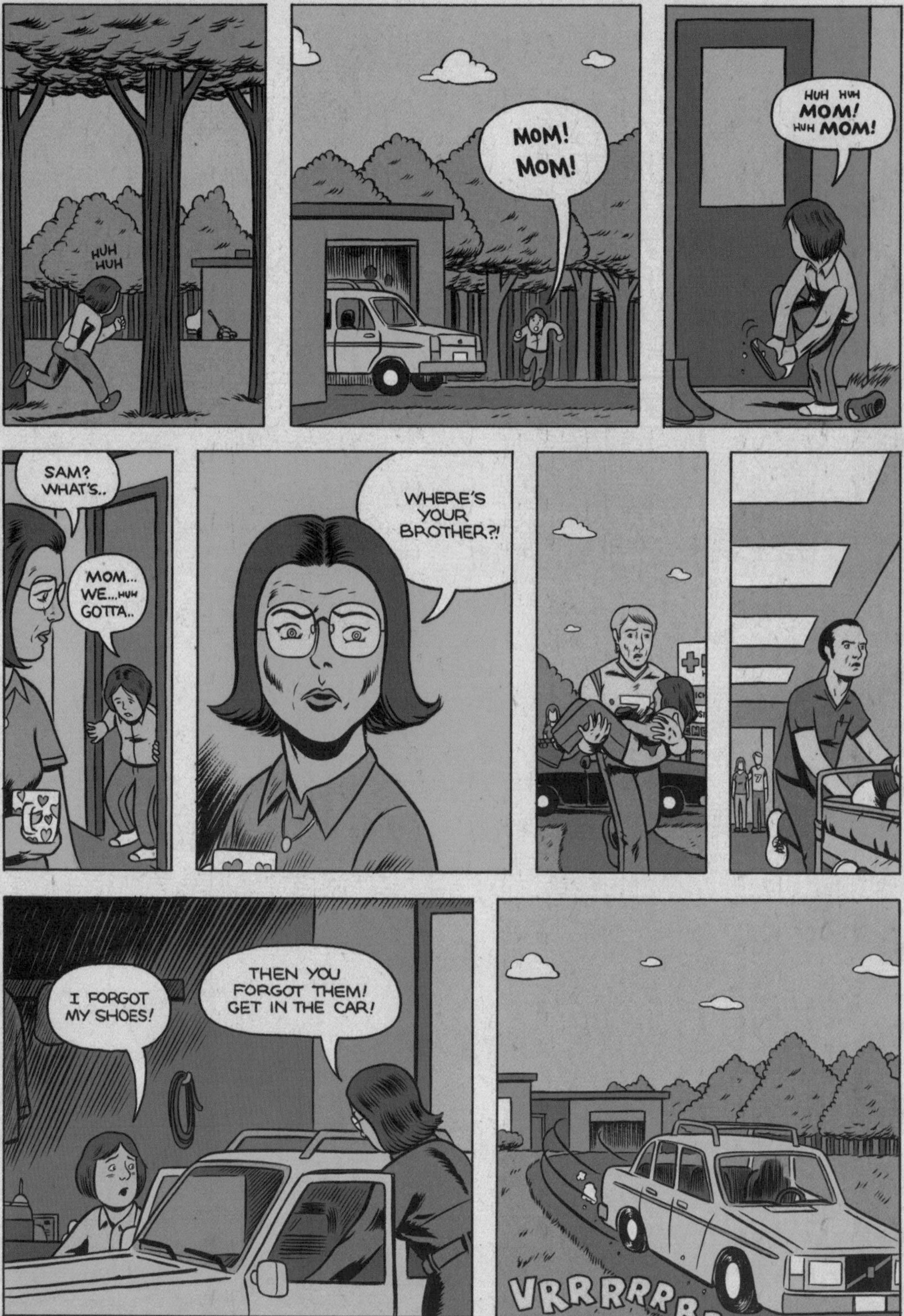
HUH HUH
MOM! MOM!
HUH HUH MOM! HUH MOM!
SAM? WHAT'S..
MOM... WE...HUH GOTTA..
WHERE'S YOUR BROTHER?!
I FORGOT MY SHOES!
THEN YOU FORGOT THEM! GET IN THE CAR!
VRRRRRR

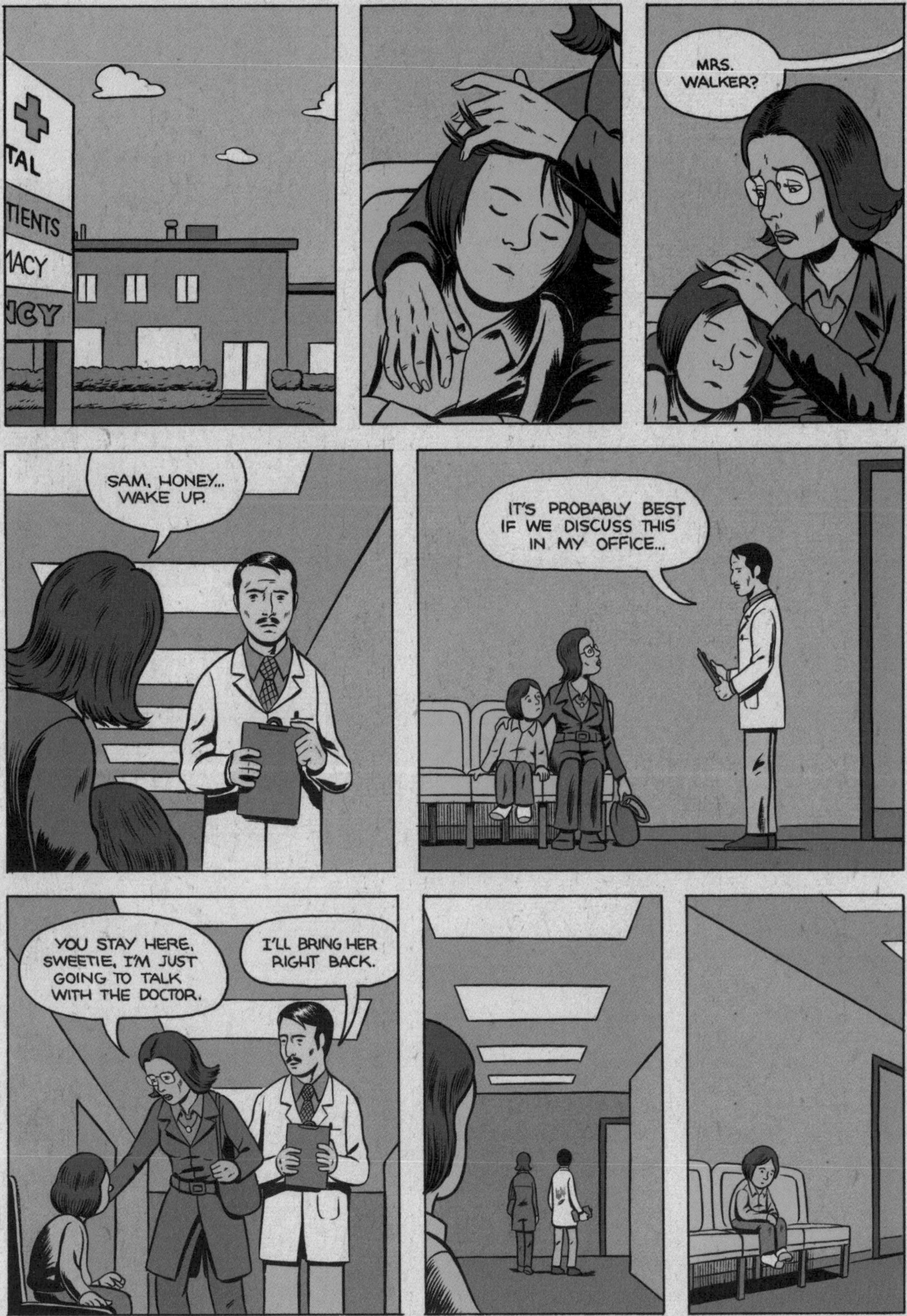
TAL
TIENTS
MACY
NCY
MRS. WALKER?
SAM, HONEY... WAKE UP.
IT'S PROBABLY BEST IF WE DISCUSS THIS IN MY OFFICE...
YOU STAY HERE, SWEETIE, I'M JUST GOING TO TALK WITH THE DOCTOR.
I'LL BRING HER RIGHT BACK.

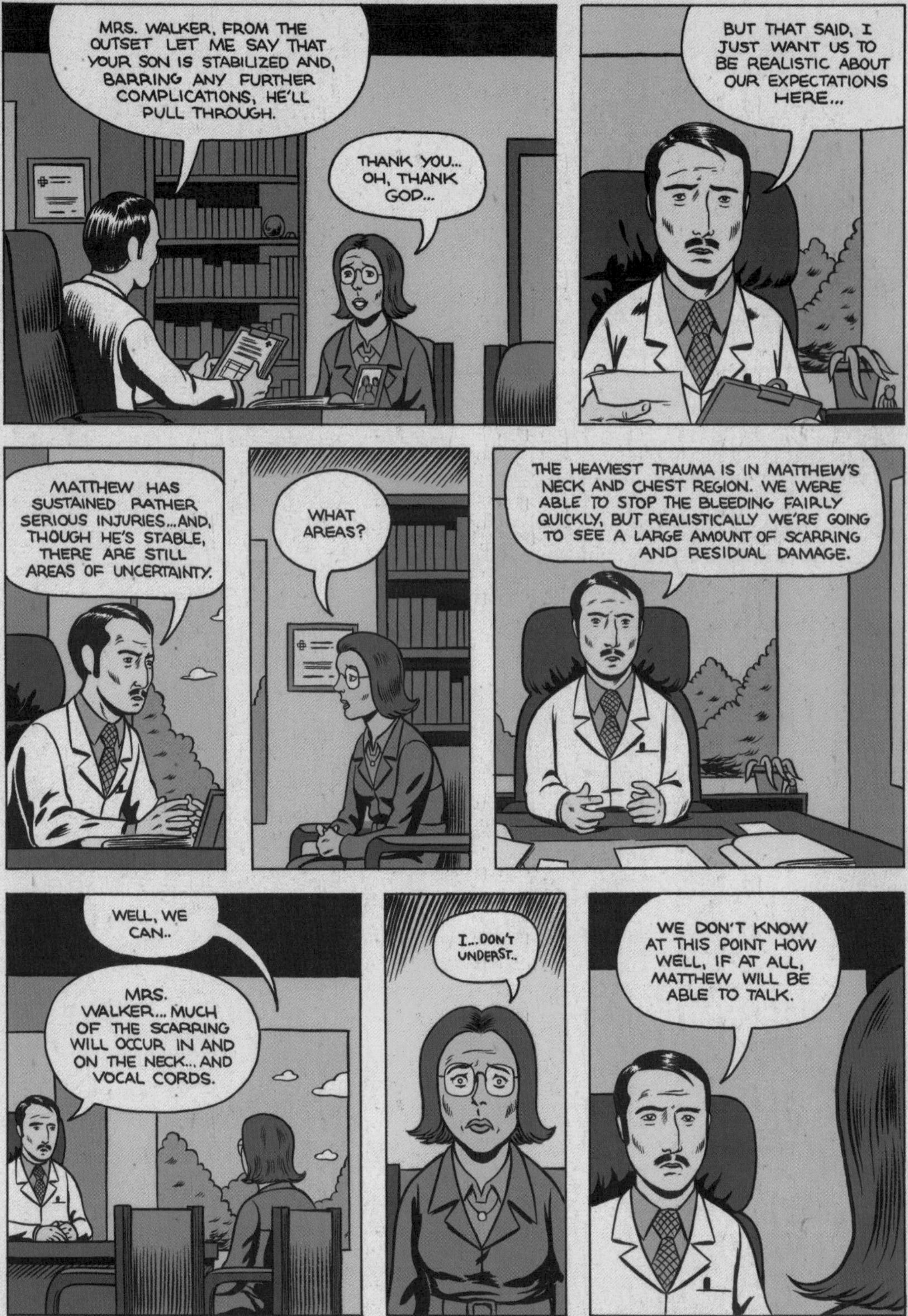
MRS. WALKER, FROM THE OUTSET LET ME SAY THAT YOUR SON IS STABILIZED AND, BARRING ANY FURTHER COMPLICATIONS, HE'LL PULL THROUGH.
THANK YOU... OH, THANK GOD...
BUT THAT SAID, I JUST WANT US TO BE REALISTIC ABOUT OUR EXPECTATIONS HERE...
MATTHEW HAS SUSTAINED RATHER SERIOUS INJURIES...AND, THOUGH HE'S STABLE, THERE ARE STILL AREAS OF UNCERTAINTY.
WHAT AREAS?
THE HEAVIEST TRAUMA IS IN MATTHEW'S NECK AND CHEST REGION. WE WERE ABLE TO STOP THE BLEEDING FAIRLY QUICKLY, BUT REALISTICALLY WE'RE GOING TO SEE A LARGE AMOUNT OF SCARRING AND RESIDUAL DAMAGE.
WELL, WE CAN..
MRS. WALKER... MUCH OF THE SCARRING WILL OCCUR IN AND ON THE NECK... AND VOCAL CORDS.
I...DON'T UNDERST..
WE DON'T KNOW AT THIS POINT HOW WELL, IF AT ALL, MATTHEW WILL BE ABLE TO TALK.

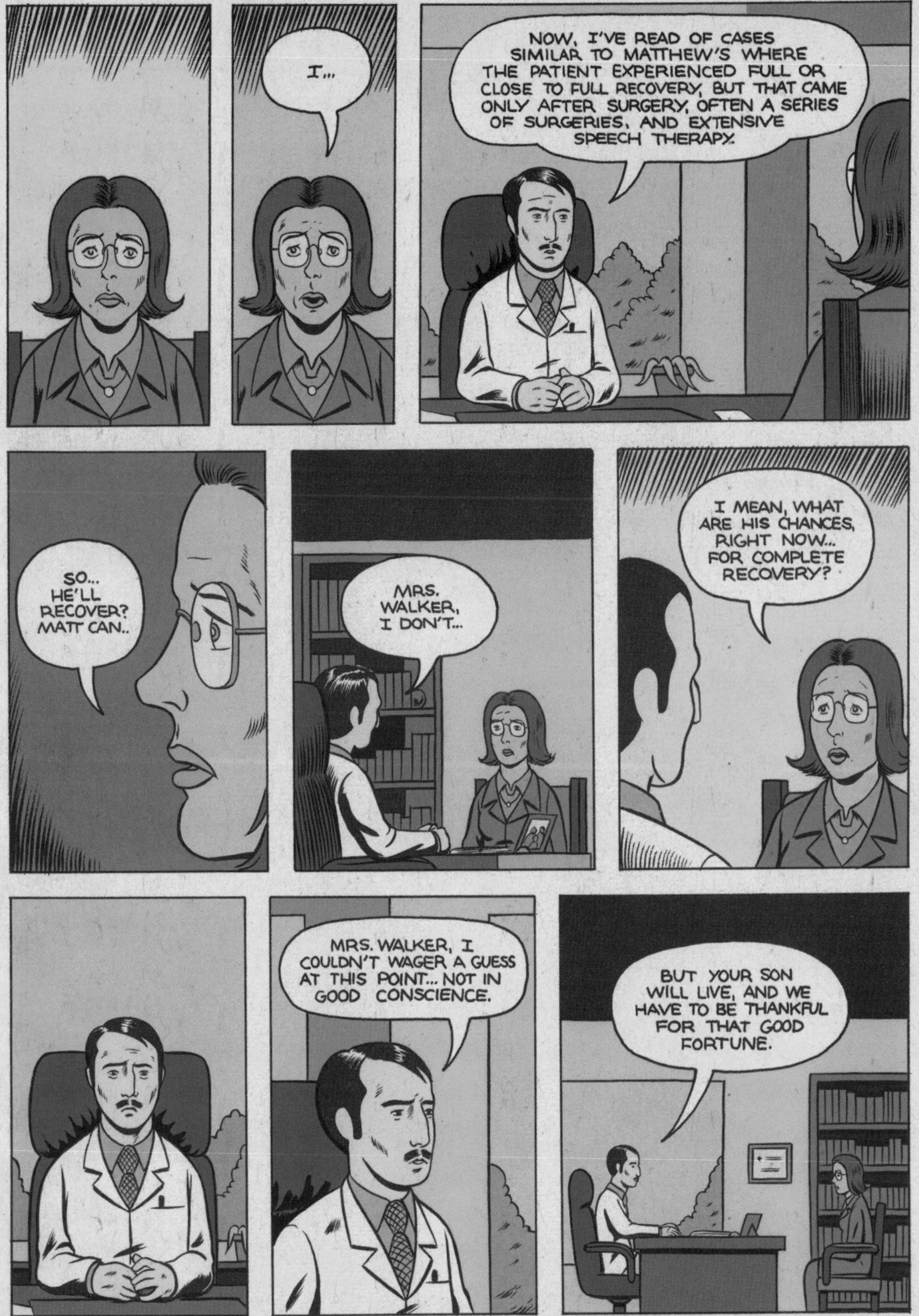
I...
NOW, I'VE READ OF CASES SIMILAR TO MATTHEW'S WHERE THE PATIENT EXPERIENCED FULL OR CLOSE TO FULL RECOVERY, BUT THAT CAME ONLY AFTER SURGERY, OFTEN A SERIES OF SURGERIES, AND EXTENSIVE SPEECH THERAPY.
SO... HE'LL RECOVER? MATT CAN..
MRS. WALKER, I DON'T...
I MEAN, WHAT ARE HIS CHANCES, RIGHT NOW... FOR COMPLETE RECOVERY?
MRS. WALKER, I COULDN'T WAGER A GUESS AT THIS POINT... NOT IN GOOD CONSCIENCE.
BUT YOUR SON WILL LIVE, AND WE HAVE TO BE THANKFUL FOR THAT GOOD FORTUNE.

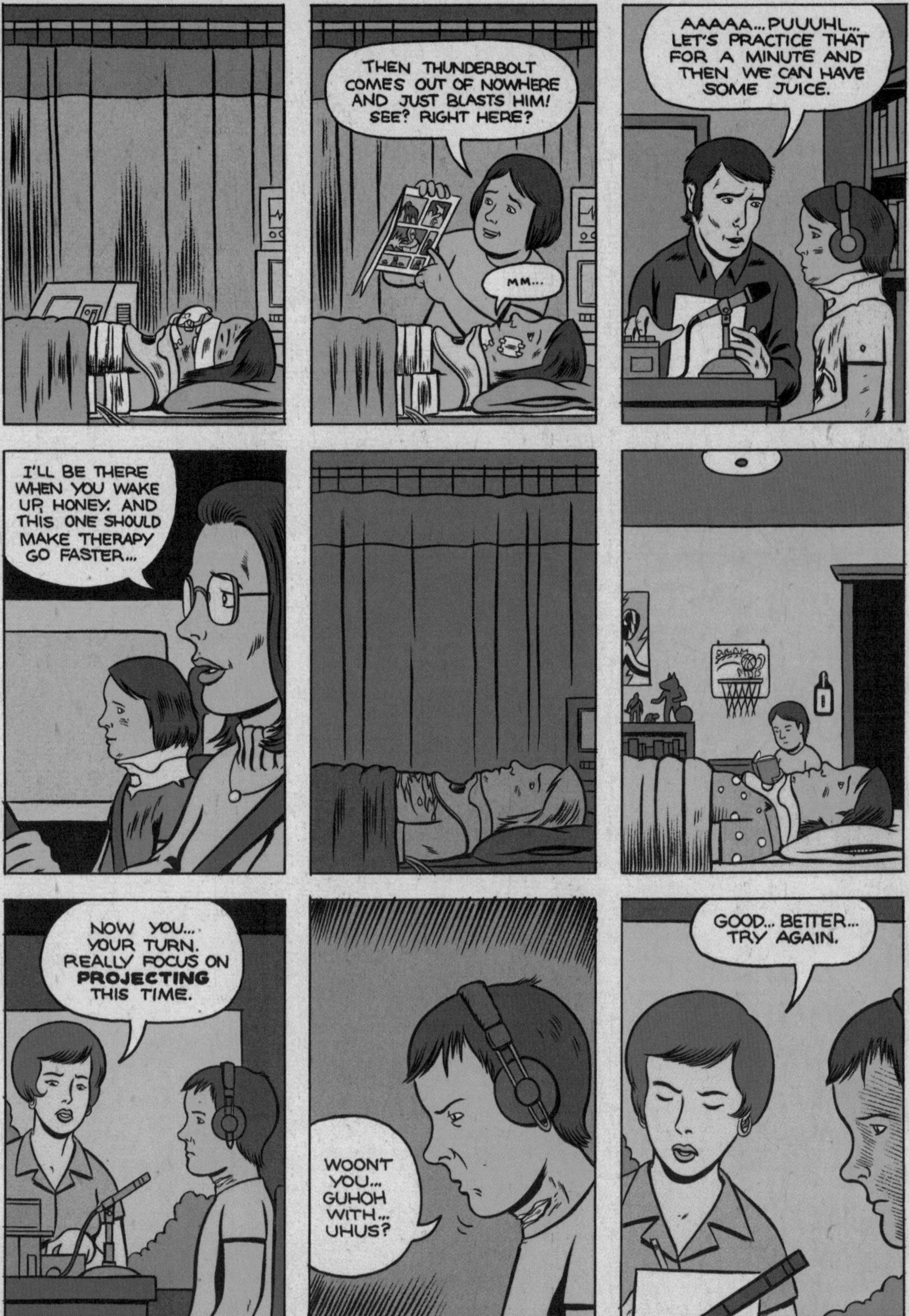
THEN THUNDERBOLT COMES OUT OF NOWHERE AND JUST BLASTS HIM! SEE? RIGHT HERE?
MM...
AAAAA... PUUUHL... LET'S PRACTICE THAT FOR A MINUTE AND THEN WE CAN HAVE SOME JUICE.
I'LL BE THERE WHEN YOU WAKE UP, HONEY. AND THIS ONE SHOULD MAKE THERAPY GO FASTER...
NOW YOU... YOUR TURN. REALLY FOCUS ON **PROJECTING** THIS TIME.
WOON'T YOU... GUHOH WITH... UHUS?
GOOD... BETTER... TRY AGAIN.

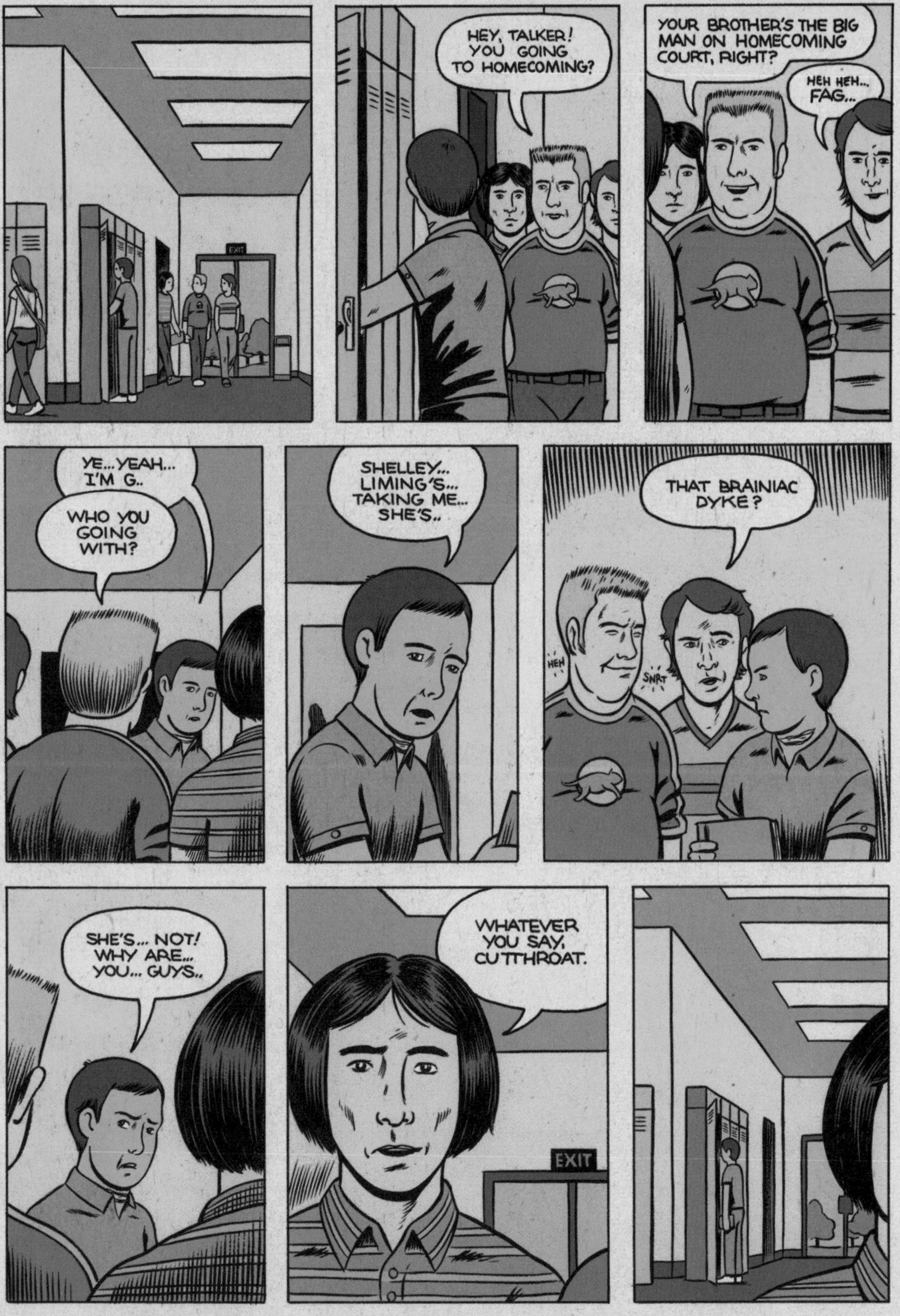
HEY, TALKER! YOU GOING TO HOMECOMING?
YOUR BROTHER'S THE BIG MAN ON HOMECOMING COURT, RIGHT?
HEH HEH... FAG...
YE... YEAH... I'M G..
WHO YOU GOING WITH?
SHELLEY... LIMING'S... TAKING ME... SHE'S..
THAT BRAINIAC DYKE?
HEH
SNRT
SHE'S... NOT! WHY ARE... YOU... GUYS..
WHATEVER YOU SAY, CUTTHROAT.
EXIT

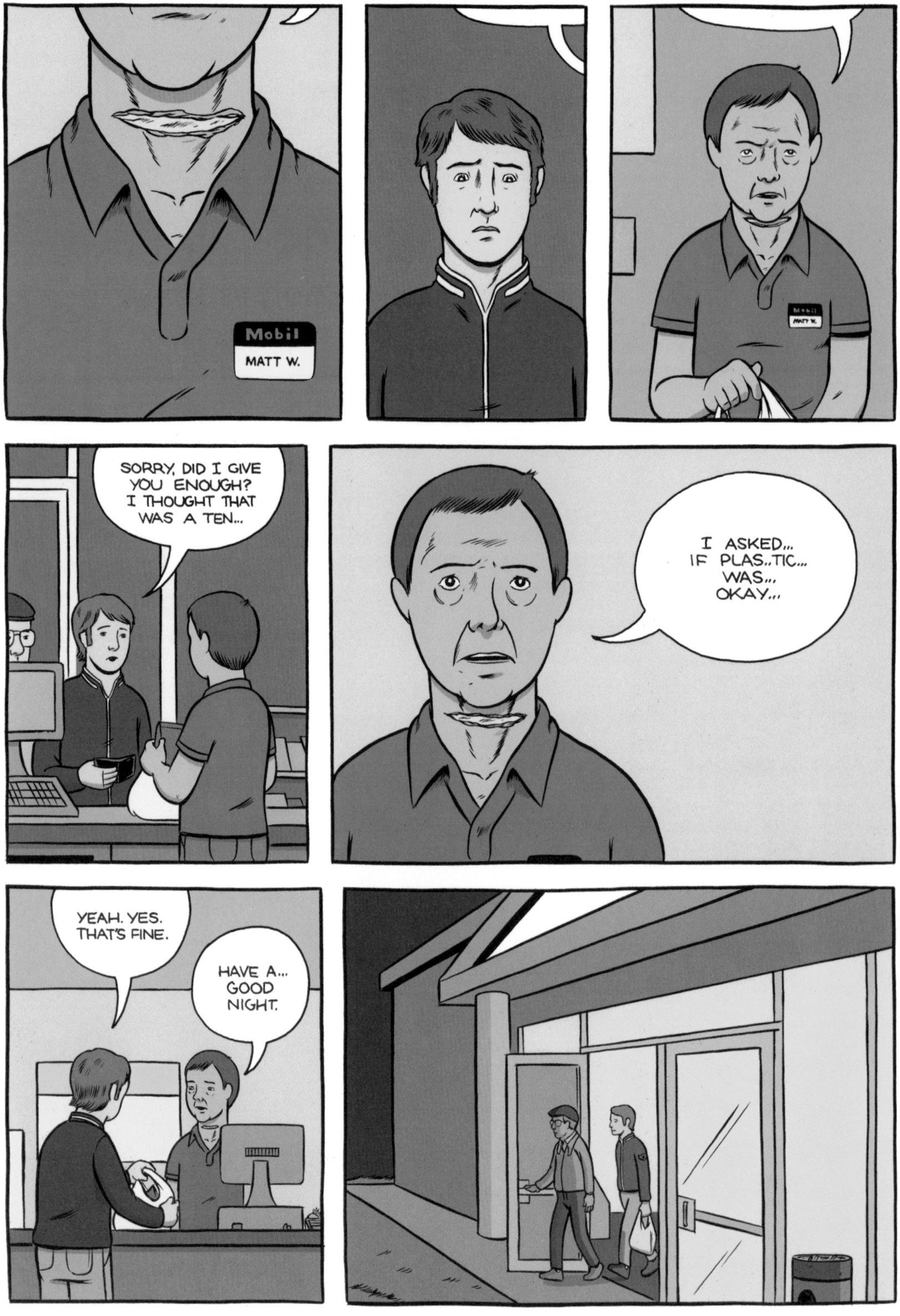
Mobil
MATT W.
Mobil
MATT W.
SORRY, DID I GIVE YOU ENOUGH? I THOUGHT THAT WAS A TEN...
I ASKED... IF PLAS..TIC... WAS... OKAY...
YEAH. YES. THAT'S FINE.
HAVE A... GOOD NIGHT.

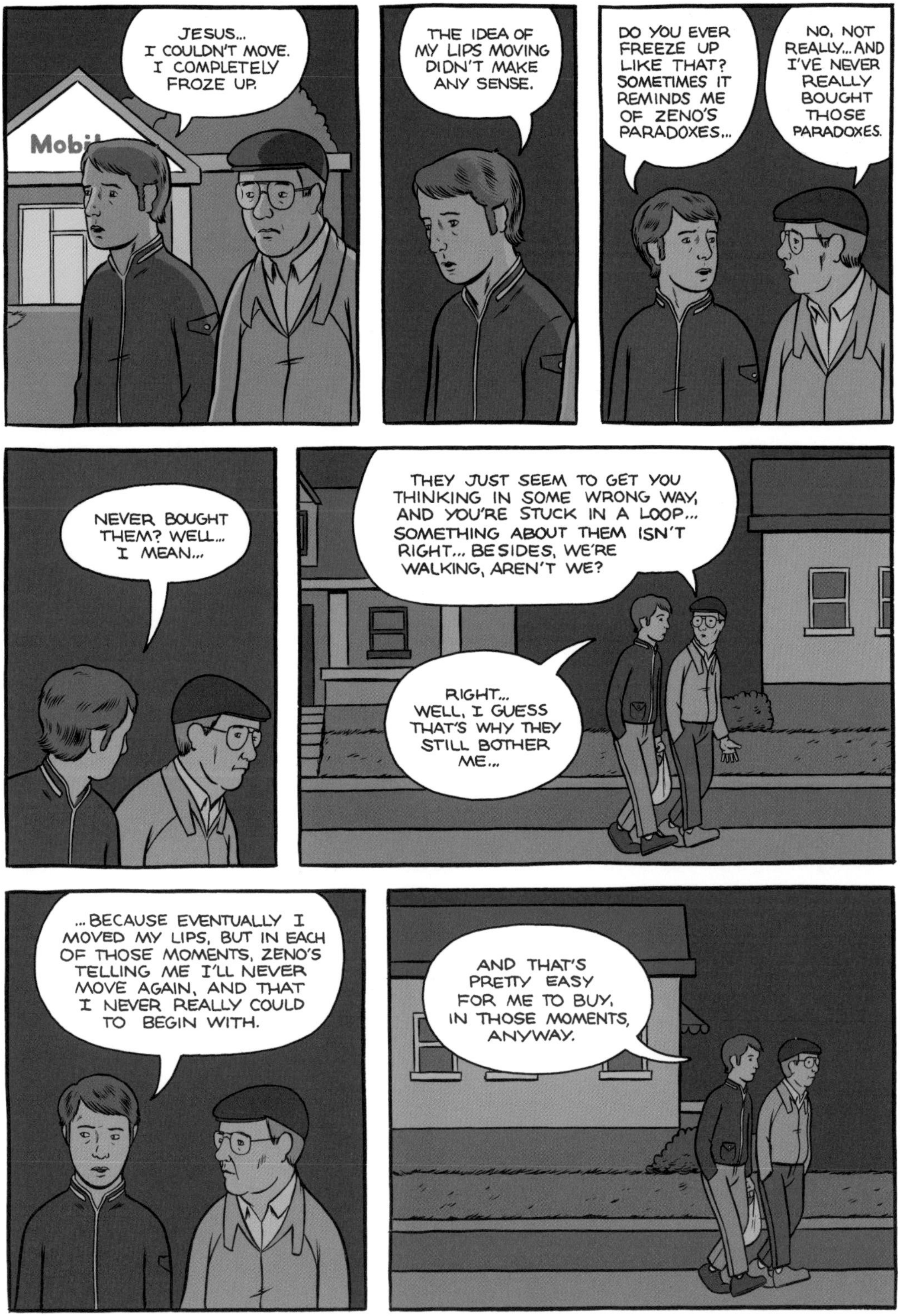
JESUS... I COULDN'T MOVE. I COMPLETELY FROZE UP.
Mobil
THE IDEA OF MY LIPS MOVING DIDN'T MAKE ANY SENSE.
DO YOU EVER FREEZE UP LIKE THAT? SOMETIMES IT REMINDS ME OF ZENO'S PARADOXES...
NO, NOT REALLY... AND I'VE NEVER REALLY BOUGHT THOSE PARADOXES.
NEVER BOUGHT THEM? WELL... I MEAN...
THEY JUST SEEM TO GET YOU THINKING IN SOME WRONG WAY, AND YOU'RE STUCK IN A LOOP... SOMETHING ABOUT THEM ISN'T RIGHT... BESIDES, WE'RE WALKING, AREN'T WE?
RIGHT... WELL, I GUESS THAT'S WHY THEY STILL BOTHER ME...
...BECAUSE EVENTUALLY I MOVED MY LIPS, BUT IN EACH OF THOSE MOMENTS, ZENO'S TELLING ME I'LL NEVER MOVE AGAIN, AND THAT I NEVER REALLY COULD TO BEGIN WITH.
AND THAT'S PRETTY EASY FOR ME TO BUY, IN THOSE MOMENTS, ANYWAY.

ELEA

JUN-JUL
Still 10¢
NO. 450

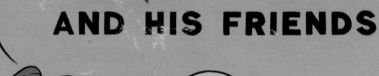

ZENO
AND HIS FRIENDS

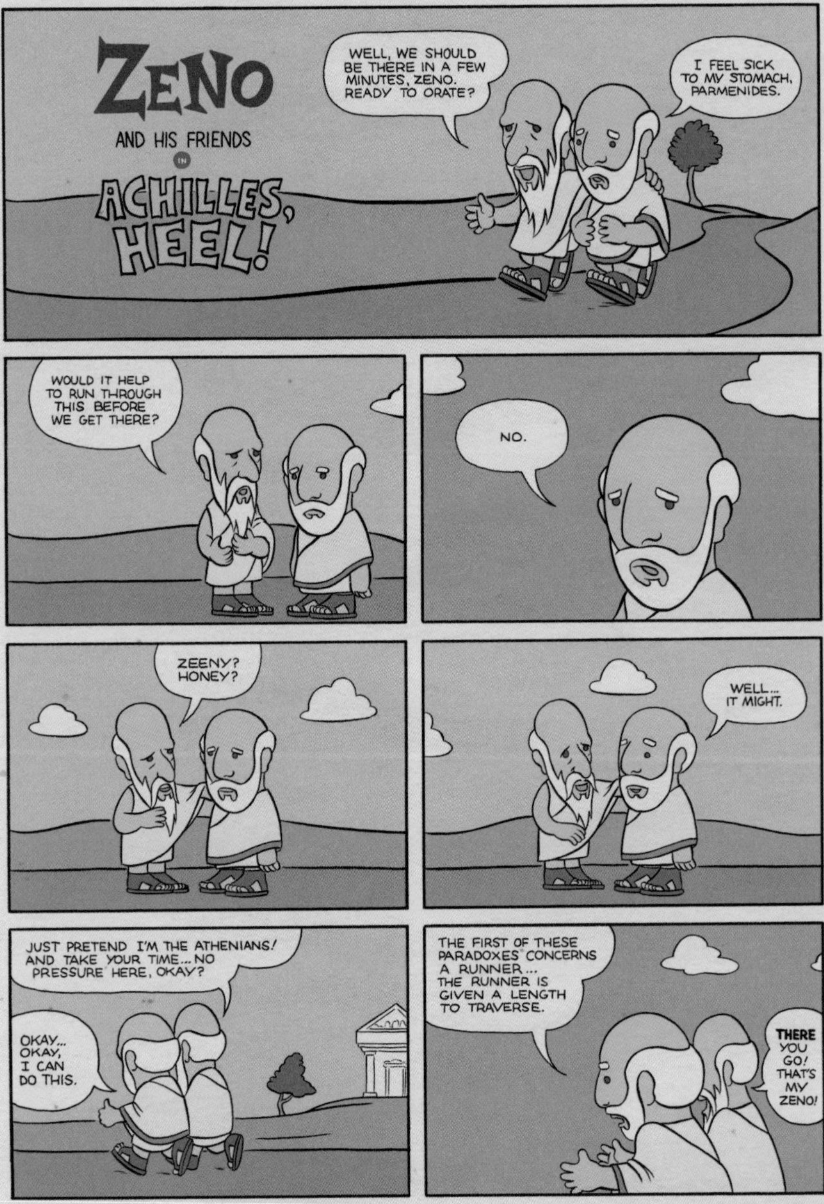
ZENO
AND HIS FRIENDS
IN
ACHILLES, HEEL!
WELL, WE SHOULD BE THERE IN A FEW MINUTES, ZENO. READY TO ORATE?
I FEEL SICK TO MY STOMACH, PARMENIDES.
WOULD IT HELP TO RUN THROUGH THIS BEFORE WE GET THERE?
NO.
ZEENY? HONEY?
WELL... IT MIGHT.
JUST PRETEND I'M THE ATHENIANS! AND TAKE YOUR TIME... NO PRESSURE HERE, OKAY?
OKAY... OKAY, I CAN DO THIS.
THE FIRST OF THESE PARADOXES CONCERNS A RUNNER... THE RUNNER IS GIVEN A LENGTH TO TRAVERSE.
THERE YOU GO! THAT'S MY ZENO!

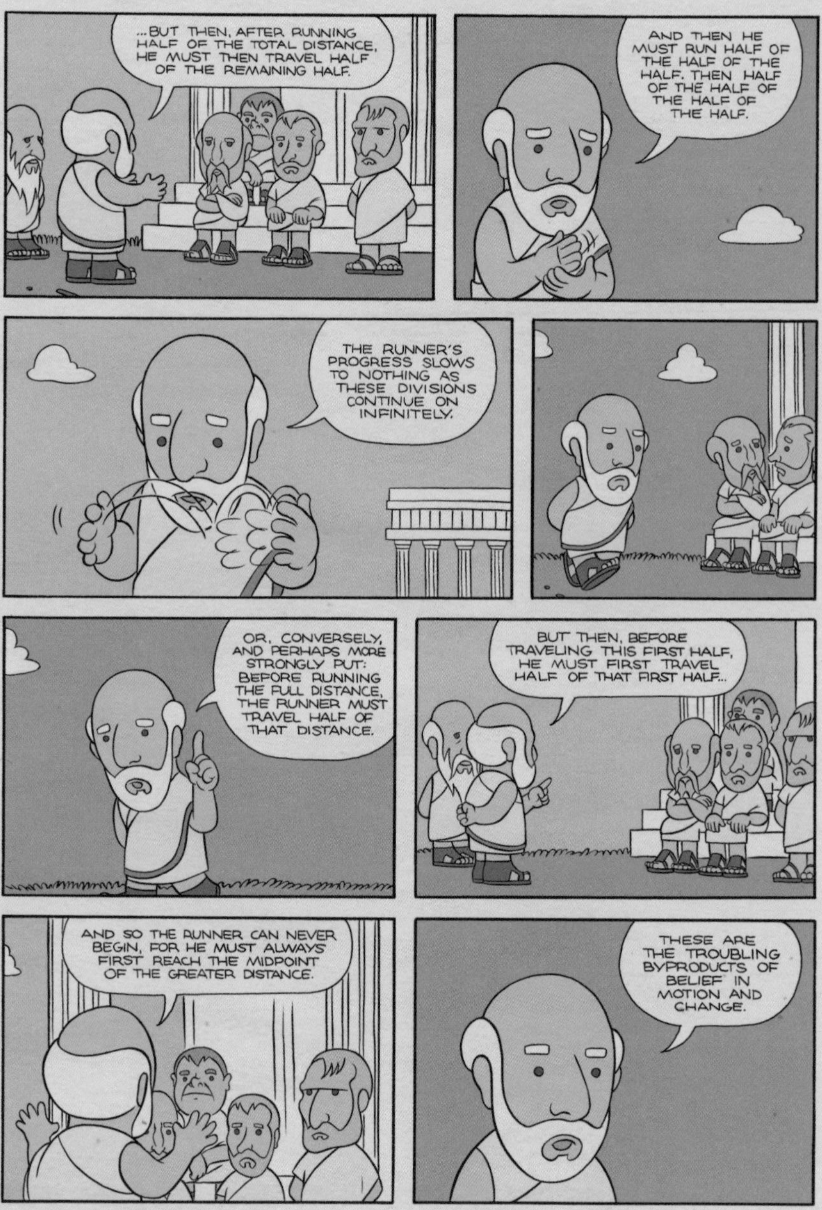
...BUT THEN, AFTER RUNNING HALF OF THE TOTAL DISTANCE, HE MUST THEN TRAVEL HALF OF THE REMAINING HALF.
AND THEN HE MUST RUN HALF OF THE HALF OF THE HALF. THEN HALF OF THE HALF OF THE HALF OF THE HALF.
THE RUNNER'S PROGRESS SLOWS TO NOTHING AS THESE DIVISIONS CONTINUE ON INFINITELY.
OR, CONVERSELY, AND PERHAPS MORE STRONGLY PUT: BEFORE RUNNING THE FULL DISTANCE, THE RUNNER MUST TRAVEL HALF OF THAT DISTANCE.
BUT THEN, BEFORE TRAVELING THIS FIRST HALF, HE MUST FIRST TRAVEL HALF OF THAT FIRST HALF...
AND SO THE RUNNER CAN NEVER BEGIN, FOR HE MUST ALWAYS FIRST REACH THE MIDPOINT OF THE GREATER DISTANCE.
THESE ARE THE TROUBLING BYPRODUCTS OF BELIEF IN MOTION AND CHANGE.

THE SECOND PARADOX IS THIS: ACHILLES, FOR ALL HIS ABILITY, CANNOT OVERTAKE A SLOWER RUNNER SOME DISTANCE AHEAD OF HIM...

FOR HE MUST FIRST REACH THAT POINT FROM WHICH THE SLOWER RUNNER STARTED, THEN REACH THE POINT WHERE THE SLOWER RUNNER WAS WHEN ACHILLES REACHED THE SLOWER MAN'S STARTING POINT. AND ON AND ON THIS GOES.

THESE SUCCESSIVE DEFICITS OF DISTANCE GO ON INFINITELY, AND OUR HERO IS FOREVER BEHIND.

THE THIRD PARADOX ¿HUNF¿ IS OF THE ARROW IN FLIGHT...

IN ANY SINGLE, INDIVISIBLE MOMENT, IS THE ARROW AT REST? OR IS IT MOVING?

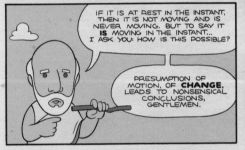

IF IT IS AT REST IN THE INSTANT, THEN IT IS NOT MOVING AND IS NEVER MOVING. BUT TO SAY IT **IS** MOVING IN THE INSTANT... I ASK YOU: HOW IS THIS POSSIBLE?

PRESUMPTION OF MOTION, OF **CHANGE**, LEADS TO NONSENSICAL CONCLUSIONS, GENTLEMEN.

THE FOURTH PARADOX I CALL "THE STADIUM," WHICH INVOLVES...

ZENO... A MOMENT ASIDE, PLEASE?

THIS LAST PARADOX...THE STADIUM? WELL, IT'S NOT THE STRONGEST. I DID MEAN TO TELL YOU BEFORE, BUT YOU WERE SO NERVOUS...

SO... JUST STICK WITH THREE?

WE CAN ALWAYS WRITE THE FOURTH DOWN LATER.

AND THOSE ARE MY PARADOXES!

WELL?
HAS NO ONE A REACTION TO ZENO'S PARADOXES?
HMM...
...
QUITE THE CONUN-DRUM...
MAN, NO OFFENSE, BUT ARE YOU GUYS RETARDED?
HERE NOW, YOUNG SOCRATES! THAT'S UNCALLED FOR!
MY BAD, BUT LOOK... LET'S JUST SAY I GO WITH YOUR THEORY, THAT CHANGE DOESN'T EXIST... THEN IT'S SCREWED RIGHT AWAY, YOU KNOW?
OKAY, LET'S SAY I DON'T KNOW YOUR THEORY, THEN YOU DEFEND IT, USING THESE PARADOXES... NOW I UNDERSTAND AND ACCEPT IT? BOOM!
HERE IN ATHENS WE CALL THAT SHIT CHANGE. CHANGE! WHAT DO THEY CALL THAT SHIT OVER IN ELEA?

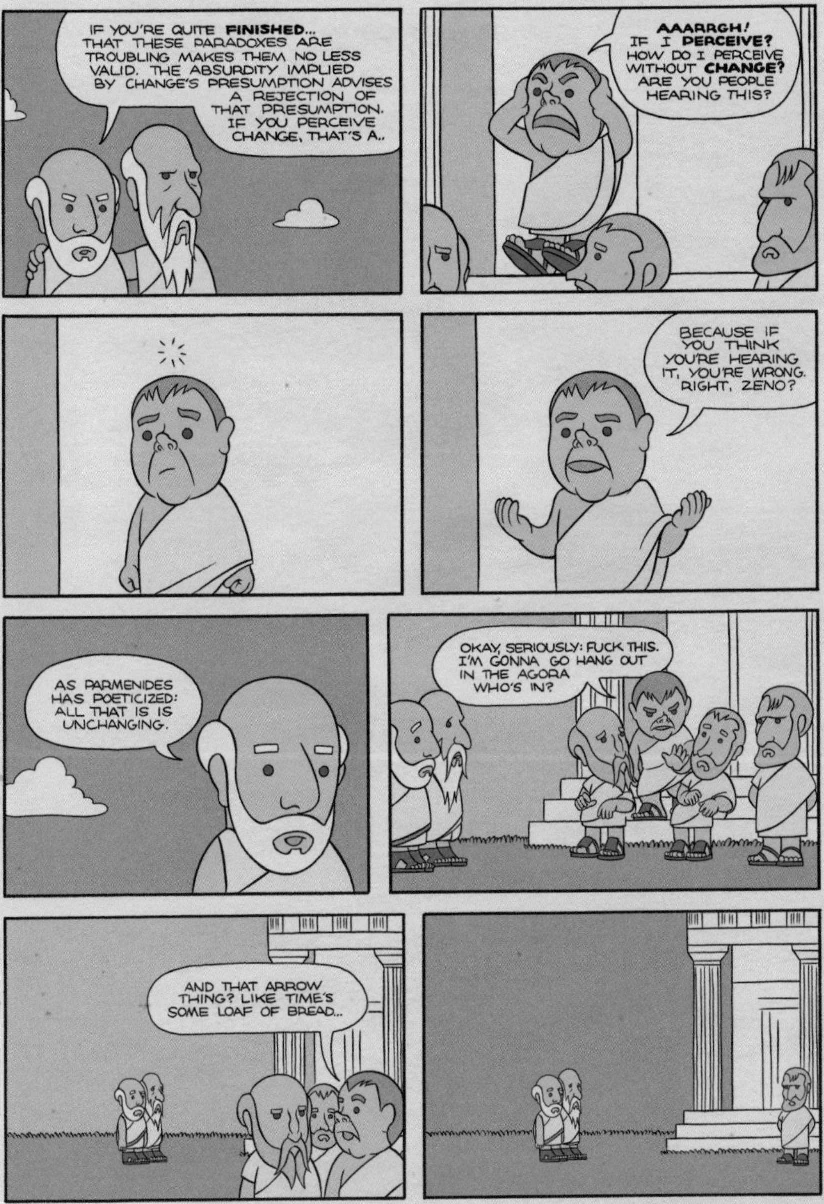
IF YOU'RE QUITE **FINISHED**... THAT THESE PARADOXES ARE TROUBLING MAKES THEM NO LESS VALID. THE ABSURDITY IMPLIED BY CHANGE'S PRESUMPTION ADVISES A REJECTION OF THAT PRESUMPTION. IF YOU PERCEIVE CHANGE, THAT'S A..
AAARRGH! IF I **PERCEIVE?** HOW DO I PERCEIVE WITHOUT **CHANGE?** ARE YOU PEOPLE HEARING THIS?
BECAUSE IF YOU THINK YOU'RE HEARING IT, YOU'RE WRONG. RIGHT, ZENO?
AS PARMENIDES HAS POETICIZED: ALL THAT IS IS UNCHANGING.
OKAY, SERIOUSLY: FUCK THIS. I'M GONNA GO HANG OUT IN THE AGORA. WHO'S IN?
AND THAT ARROW THING? LIKE TIME'S SOME LOAF OF BREAD...

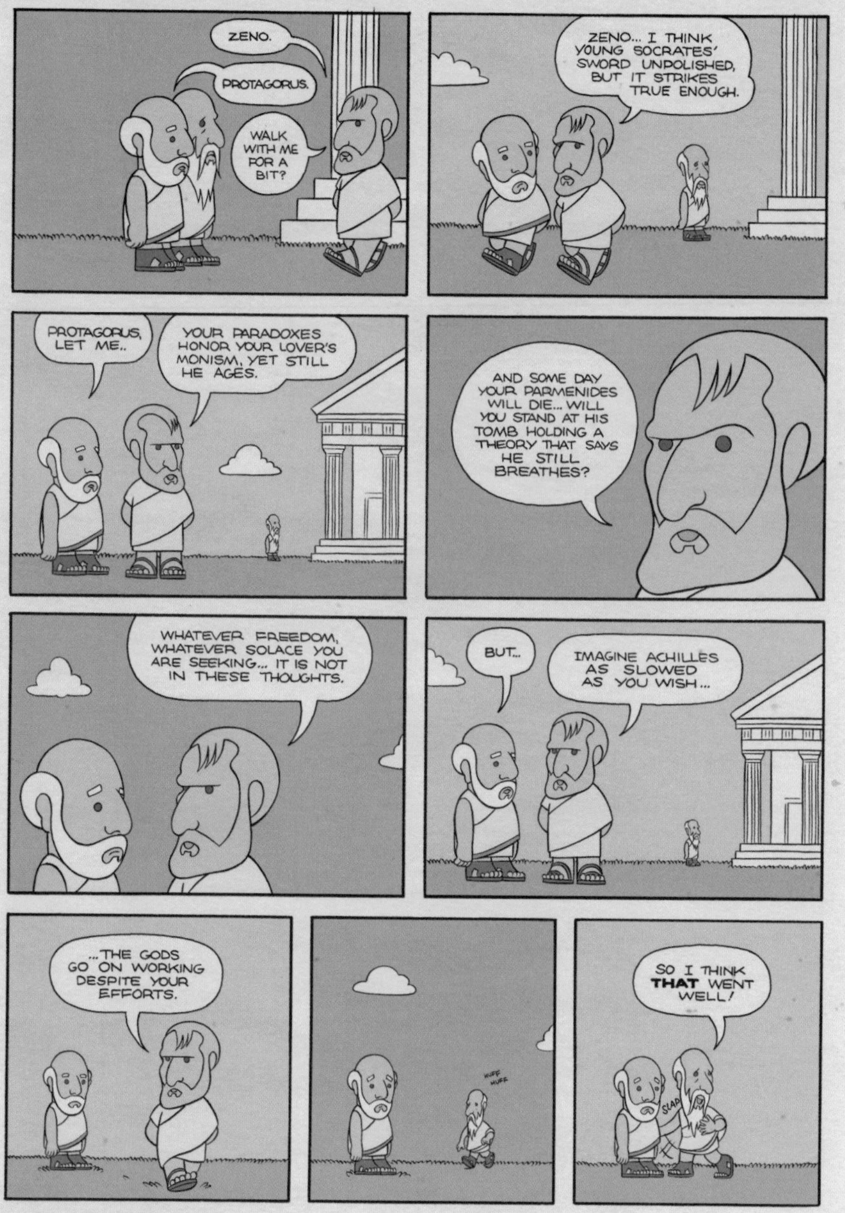
ZENO.
PROTAGORUS.
WALK WITH ME FOR A BIT?
ZENO... I THINK YOUNG SOCRATES' SWORD UNPOLISHED, BUT IT STRIKES TRUE ENOUGH.
PROTAGORUS, LET ME..
YOUR PARADOXES HONOR YOUR LOVER'S MONISM, YET STILL HE AGES.
AND SOME DAY YOUR PARMENIDES WILL DIE... WILL YOU STAND AT HIS TOMB HOLDING A THEORY THAT SAYS HE STILL BREATHES?
WHATEVER FREEDOM, WHATEVER SOLACE YOU ARE SEEKING... IT IS NOT IN THESE THOUGHTS.
BUT...
IMAGINE ACHILLES AS SLOWED AS YOU WISH...
...THE GODS GO ON WORKING DESPITE YOUR EFFORTS.
HUFF HUFF
SO I THINK **THAT** WENT WELL!
SLAP

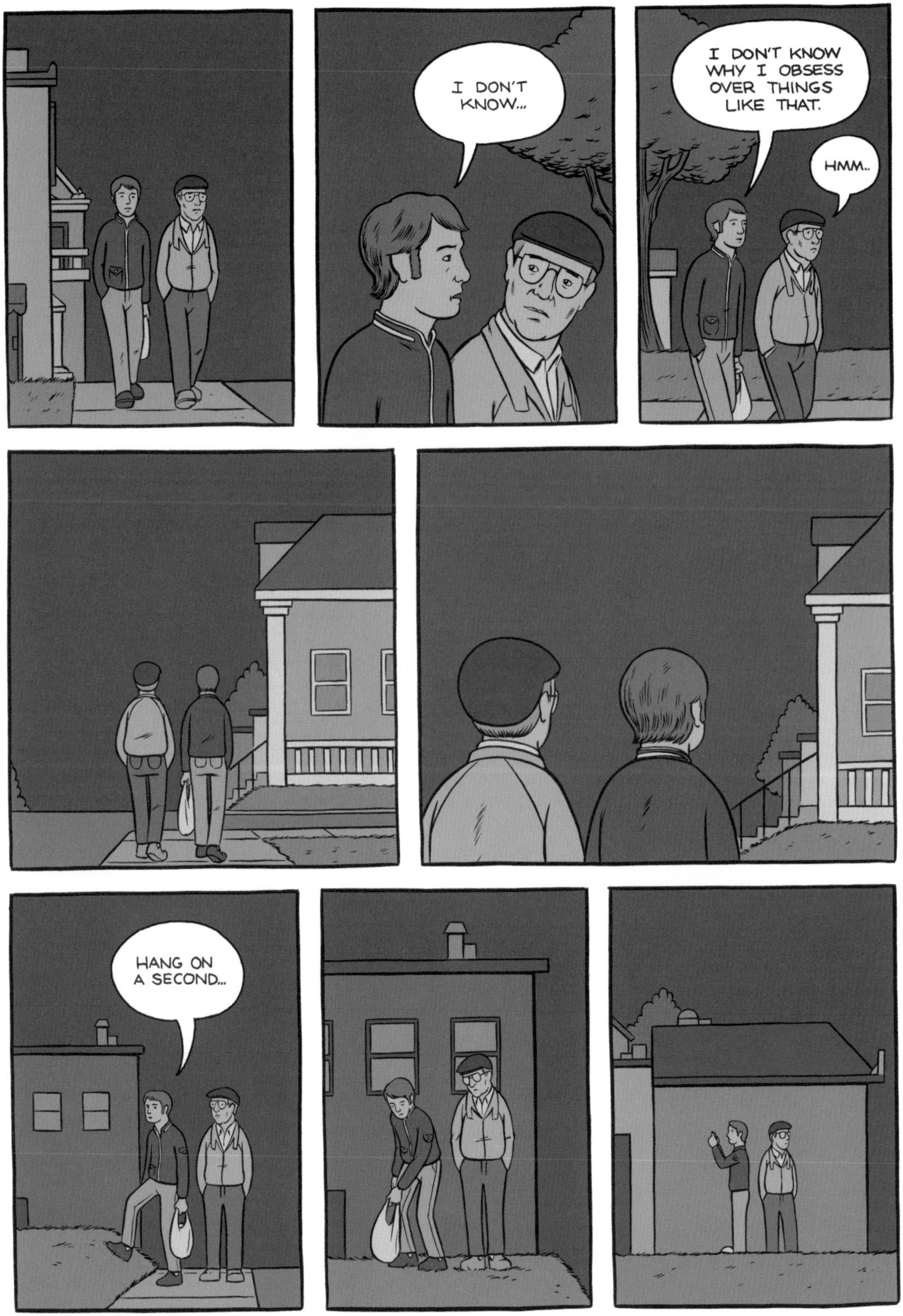
I DON'T KNOW...
I DON'T KNOW WHY I OBSESS OVER THINGS LIKE THAT.
HMM..
HANG ON A SECOND...

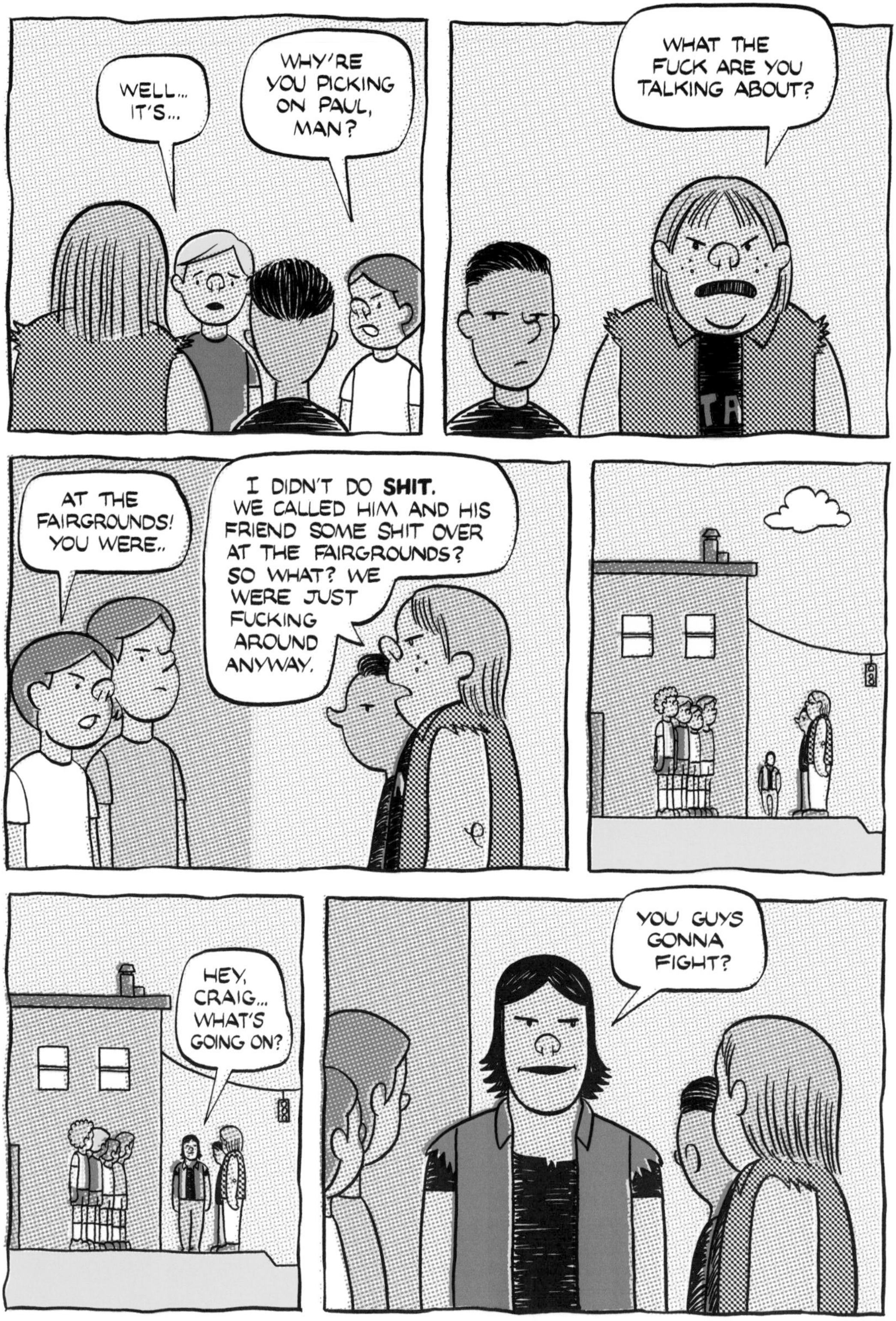
WELL... IT'S...
WHY'RE YOU PICKING ON PAUL, MAN?
WHAT THE FUCK ARE YOU TALKING ABOUT?
TA
AT THE FAIRGROUNDS! YOU WERE..
I DIDN'T DO SHIT. WE CALLED HIM AND HIS FRIEND SOME SHIT OVER AT THE FAIRGROUNDS? SO WHAT? WE WERE JUST FUCKING AROUND ANYWAY.
HEY, CRAIG... WHAT'S GOING ON?
YOU GUYS GONNA FIGHT?

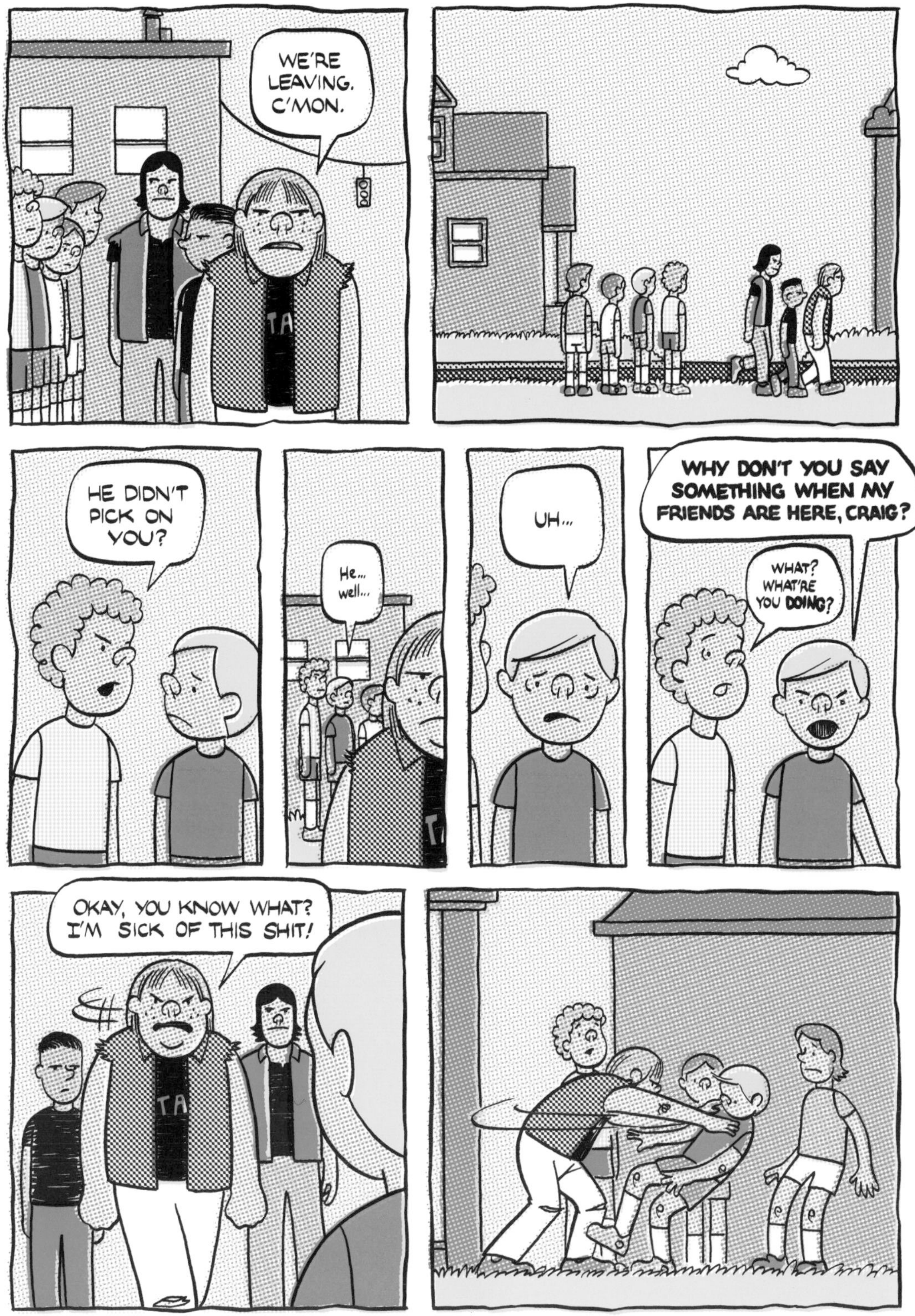
WE'RE LEAVING. C'MON.
HE DIDN'T PICK ON YOU?
He... well...
UH...
WHY DON'T YOU SAY SOMETHING WHEN MY FRIENDS ARE HERE, CRAIG?
WHAT? WHAT'RE YOU DOING?
OKAY, YOU KNOW WHAT? I'M SICK OF THIS SHIT!

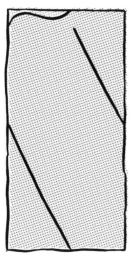

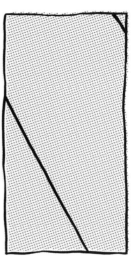

ANYBODY STEPS IN, I'LL KICK YOUR ASS. IT'S BETWEEN THEM TWO, SO BACK OFF.

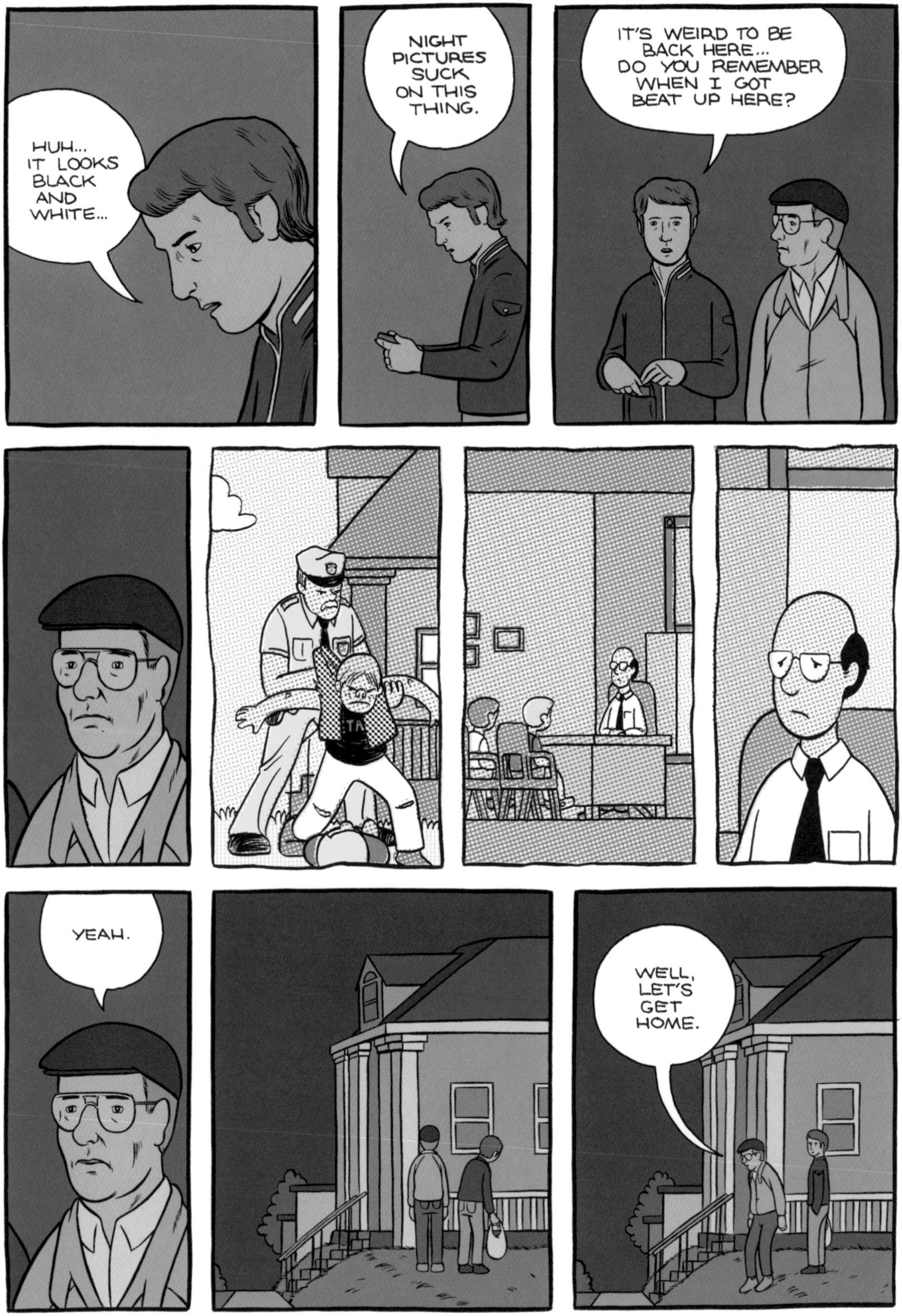
HUH... IT LOOKS BLACK AND WHITE...
NIGHT PICTURES SUCK ON THIS THING.
IT'S WEIRD TO BE BACK HERE... DO YOU REMEMBER WHEN I GOT BEAT UP HERE?
YEAH.
WELL, LET'S GET HOME.

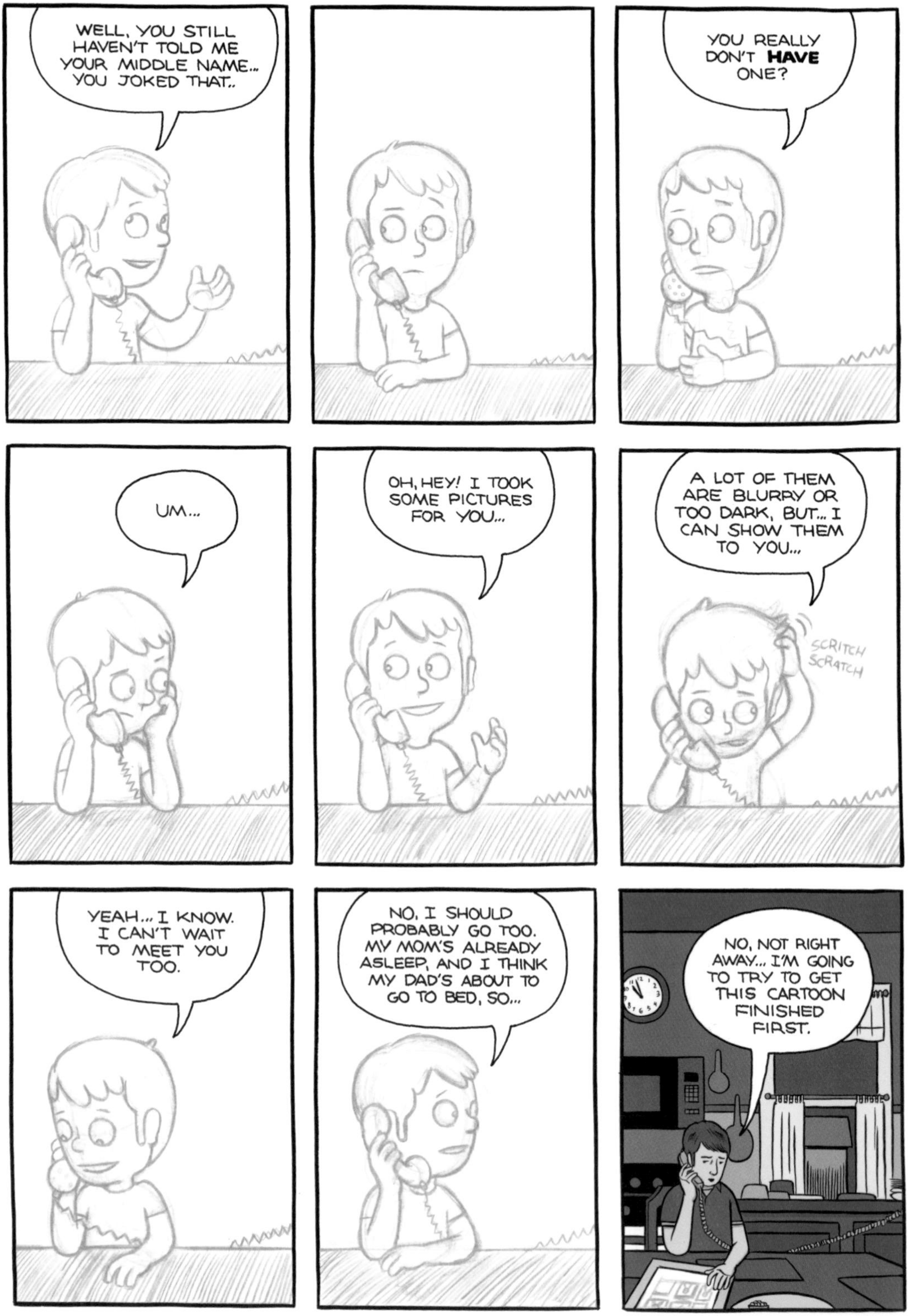
WELL, YOU STILL HAVEN'T TOLD ME YOUR MIDDLE NAME... YOU JOKED THAT..
YOU REALLY DON'T **HAVE** ONE?
UM...
OH, HEY! I TOOK SOME PICTURES FOR YOU...
A LOT OF THEM ARE BLURRY OR TOO DARK, BUT... I CAN SHOW THEM TO YOU...
SCRITCH SCRATCH
YEAH... I KNOW. I CAN'T WAIT TO MEET YOU TOO.
NO, I SHOULD PROBABLY GO TOO. MY MOM'S ALREADY ASLEEP, AND I THINK MY DAD'S ABOUT TO GO TO BED, SO...
NO, NOT RIGHT AWAY... I'M GOING TO TRY TO GET THIS CARTOON FINISHED FIRST.

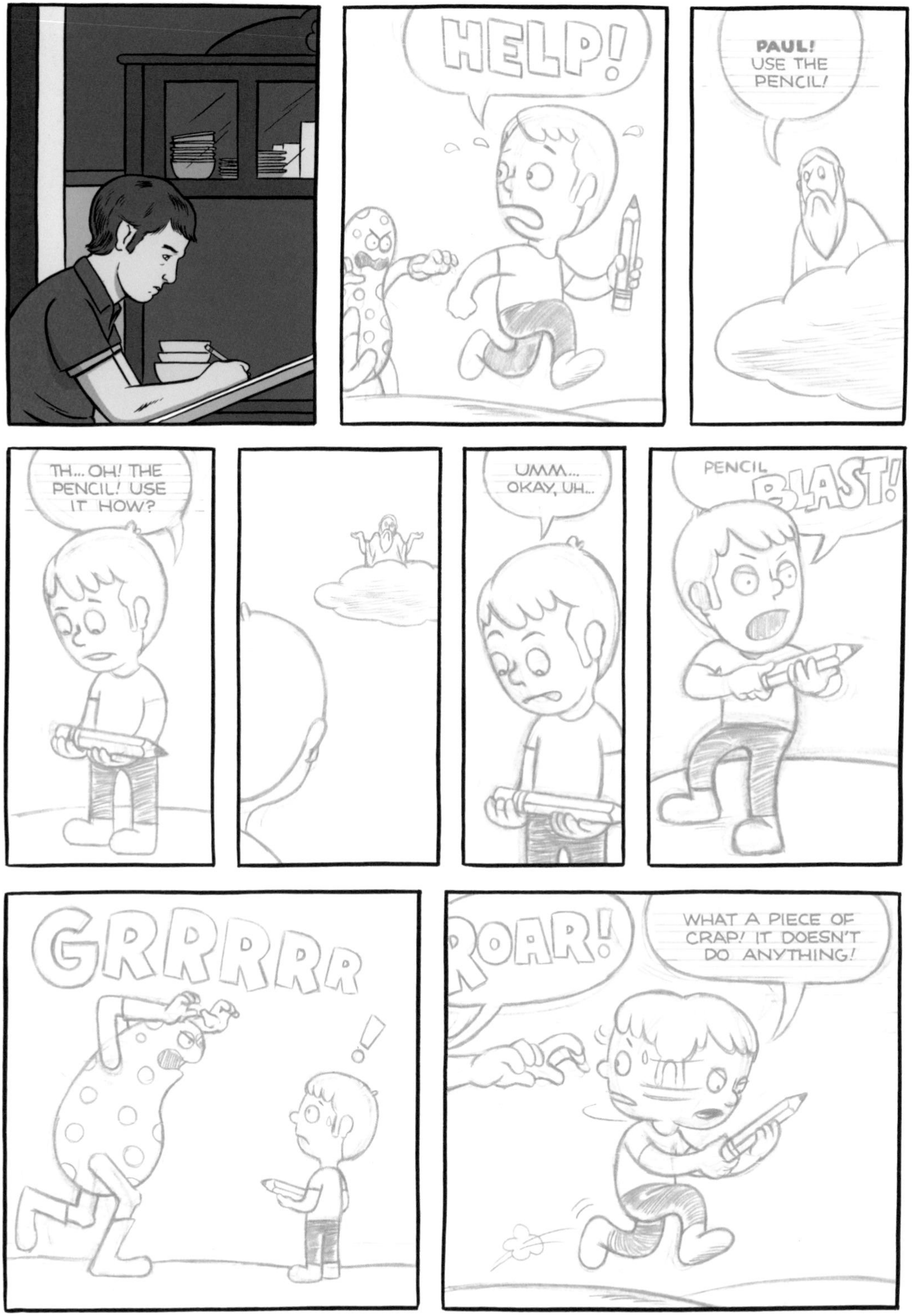
HELP!
PAUL! USE THE PENCIL!
TH... OH! THE PENCIL! USE IT HOW?
UMM... OKAY, UH...
PENCIL BLAST!
GRRRRR
!
ROAR!
WHAT A PIECE OF CRAP! IT DOESN'T DO ANYTHING!

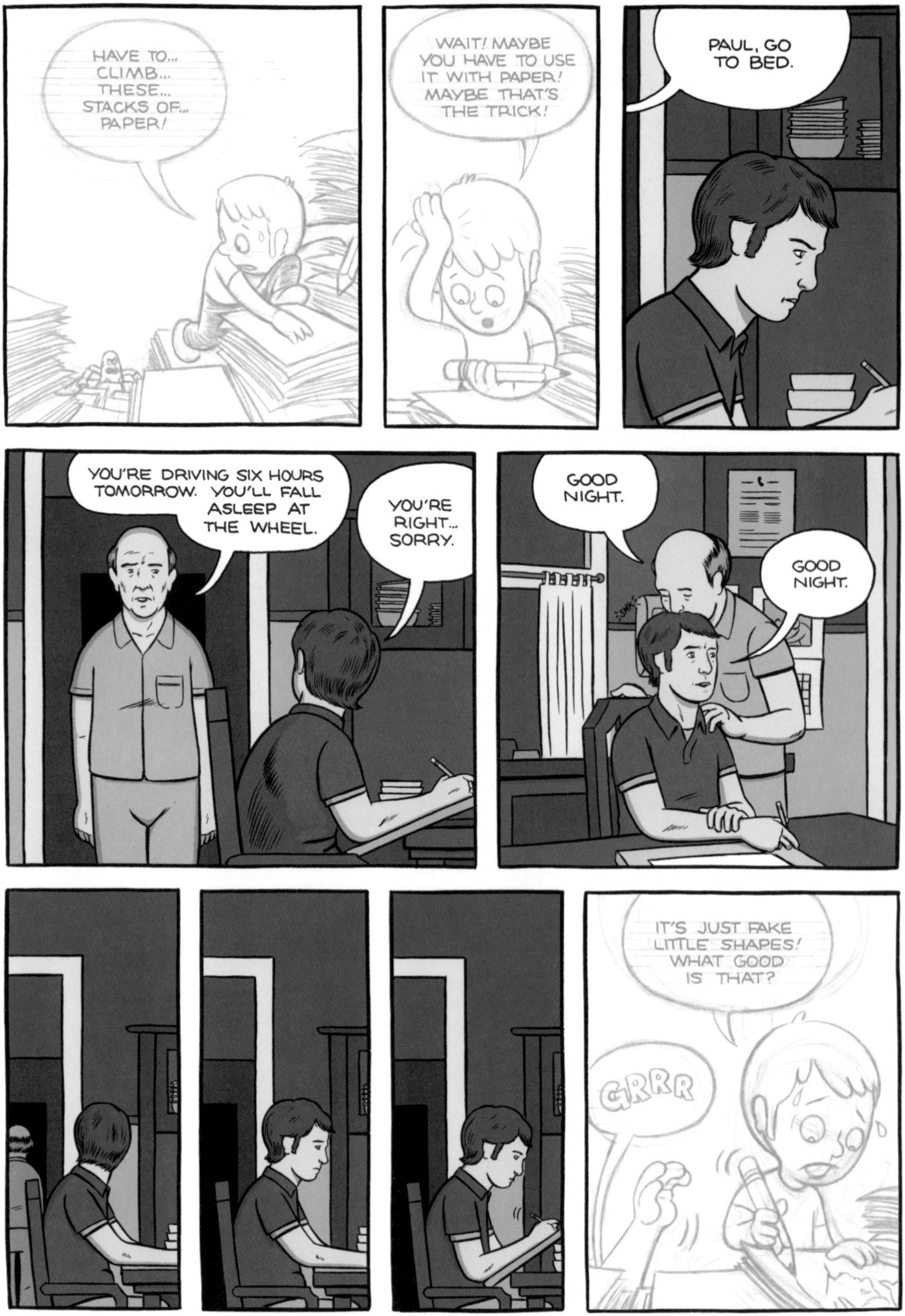
HAVE TO... CLIMB... THESE... STACKS OF... PAPER!
WAIT! MAYBE YOU HAVE TO USE IT WITH PAPER! MAYBE THAT'S THE TRICK!
PAUL, GO TO BED.
YOU'RE DRIVING SIX HOURS TOMORROW. YOU'LL FALL ASLEEP AT THE WHEEL.
YOU'RE RIGHT... SORRY.
GOOD NIGHT.
SMK
GOOD NIGHT.
IT'S JUST FAKE LITTLE SHAPES! WHAT GOOD IS THAT?
GRRR

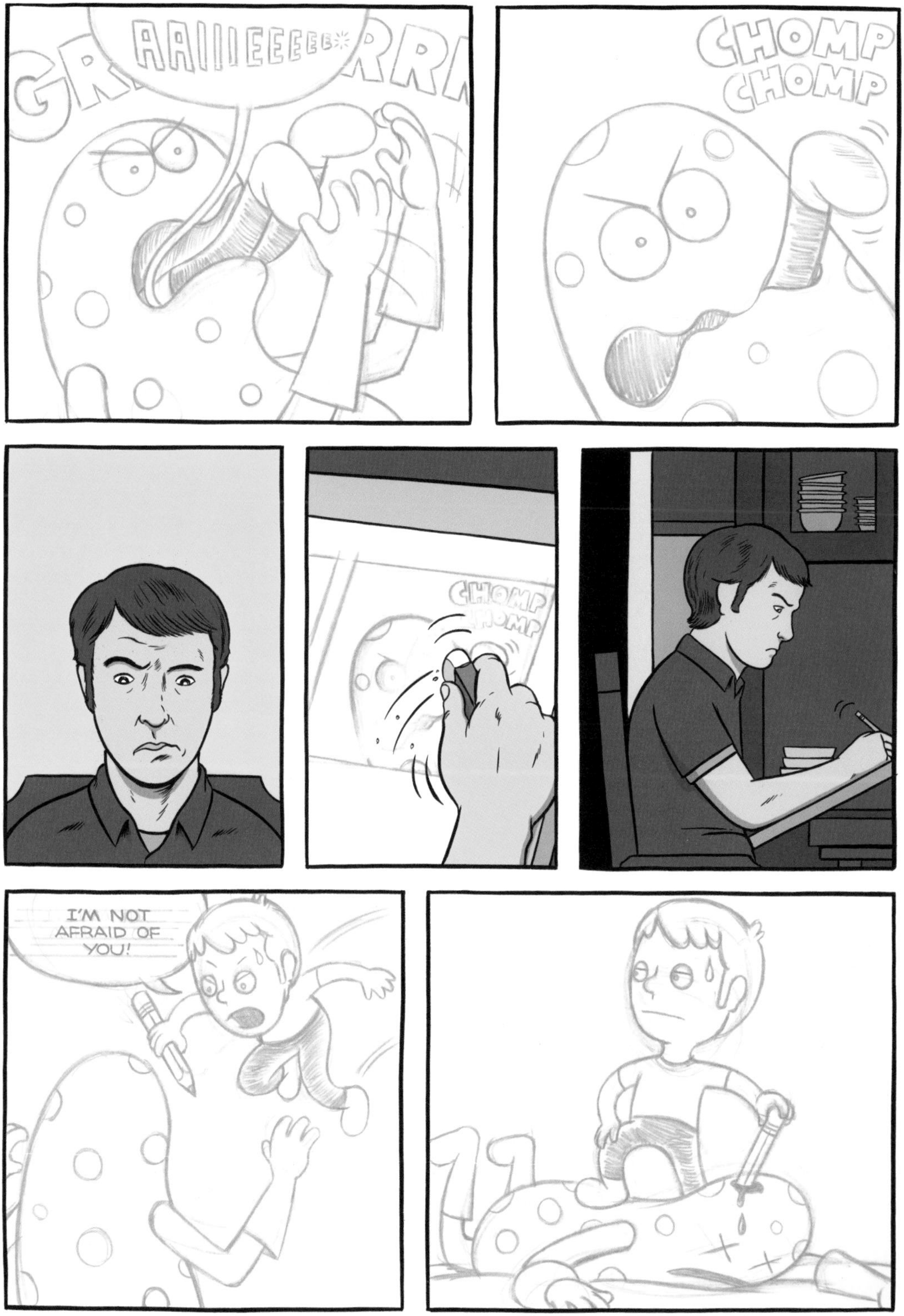
GRRRR
AAIIIEEEEE
CHOMP CHOMP
CHOMP CHOMP
I'M NOT AFRAID OF YOU!

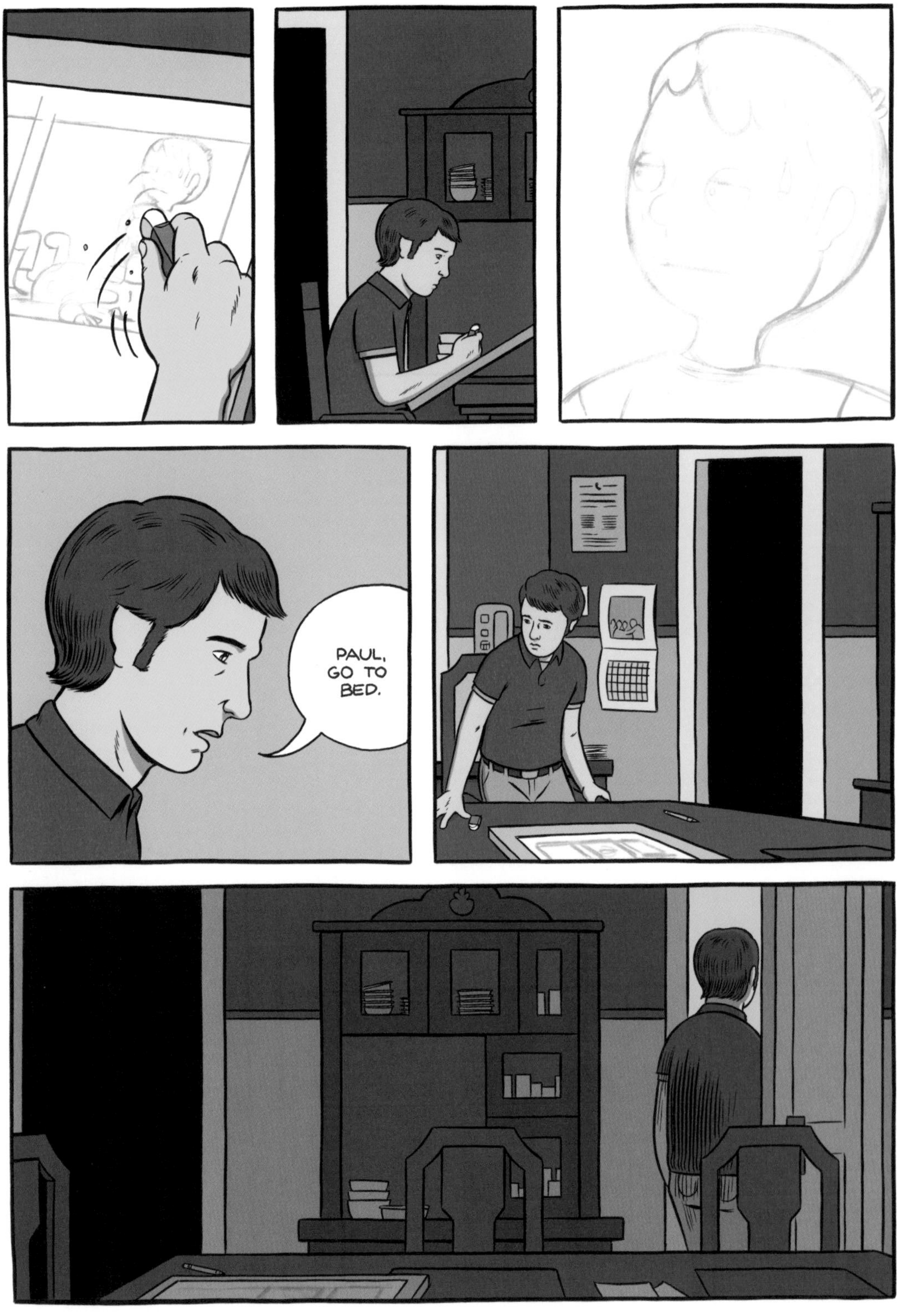
PAUL,
GO TO
BED.

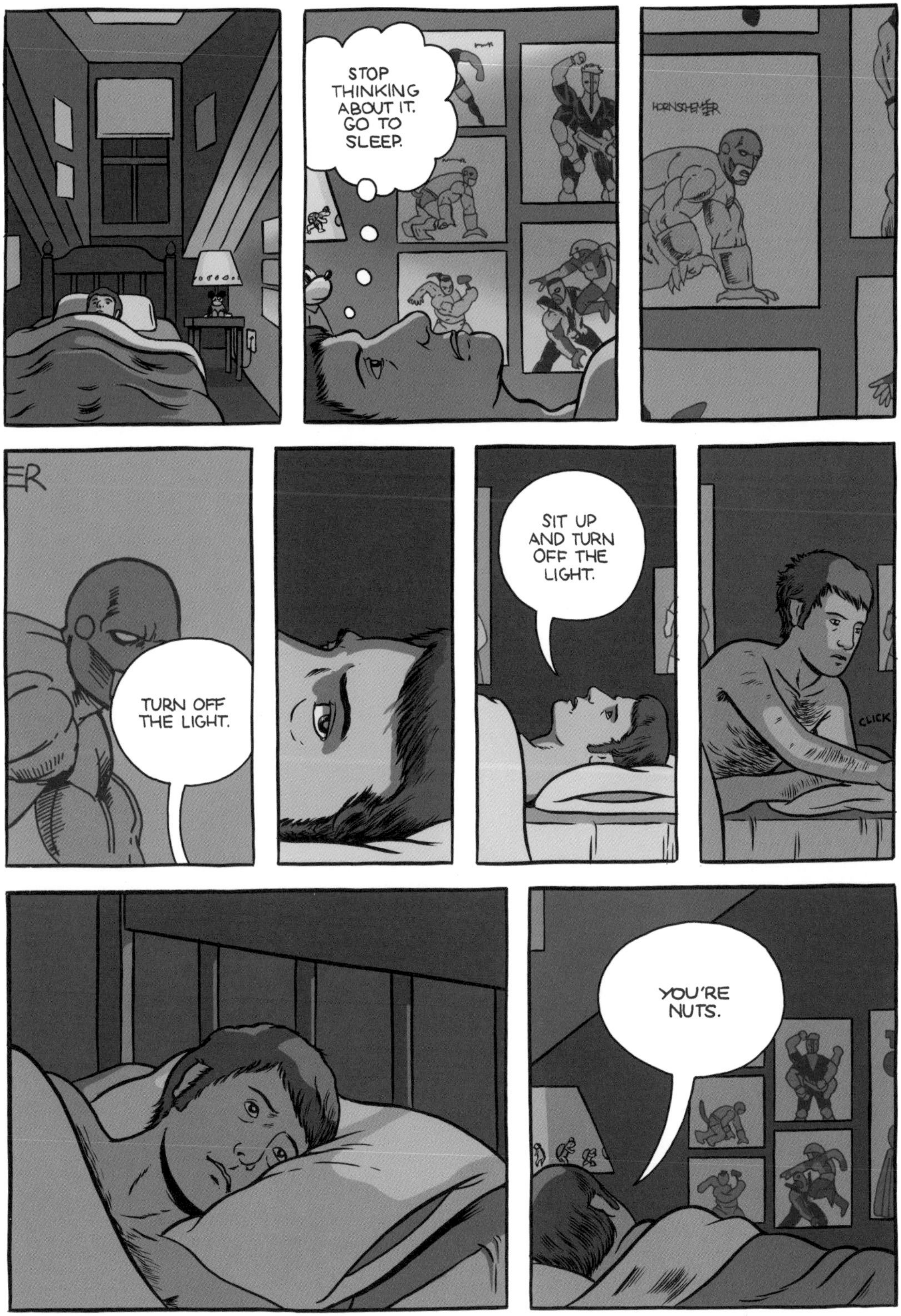
STOP THINKING ABOUT IT. GO TO SLEEP.
HORNSCHEMEIER
TURN OFF THE LIGHT.
SIT UP AND TURN OFF THE LIGHT.
CLICK
YOU'RE NUTS.

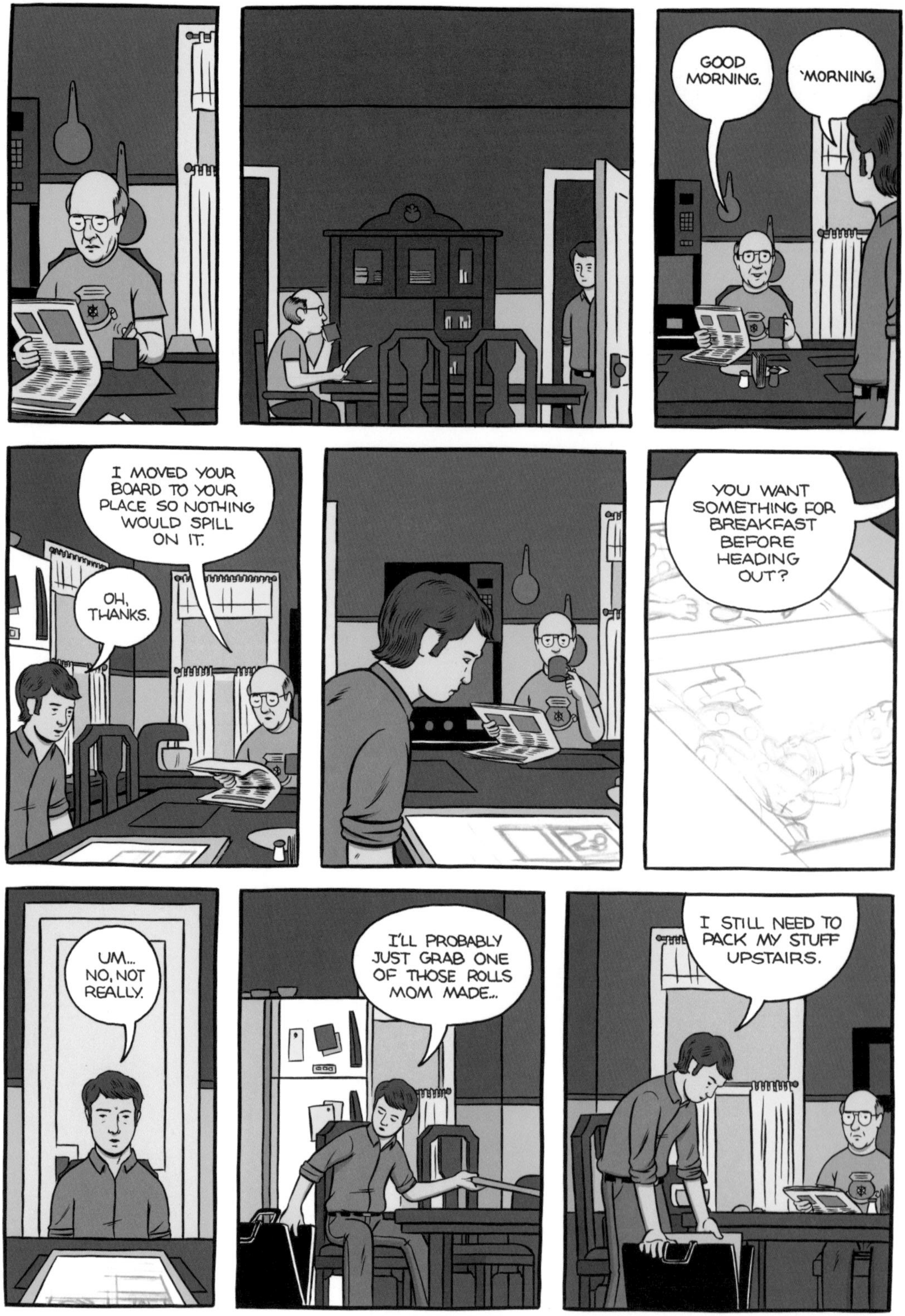
GOOD MORNING.
`MORNING.
I MOVED YOUR BOARD TO YOUR PLACE SO NOTHING WOULD SPILL ON IT.
OH, THANKS.
YOU WANT SOMETHING FOR BREAKFAST BEFORE HEADING OUT?
UM... NO, NOT REALLY.
I'LL PROBABLY JUST GRAB ONE OF THOSE ROLLS MOM MADE...
I STILL NEED TO PACK MY STUFF UPSTAIRS.

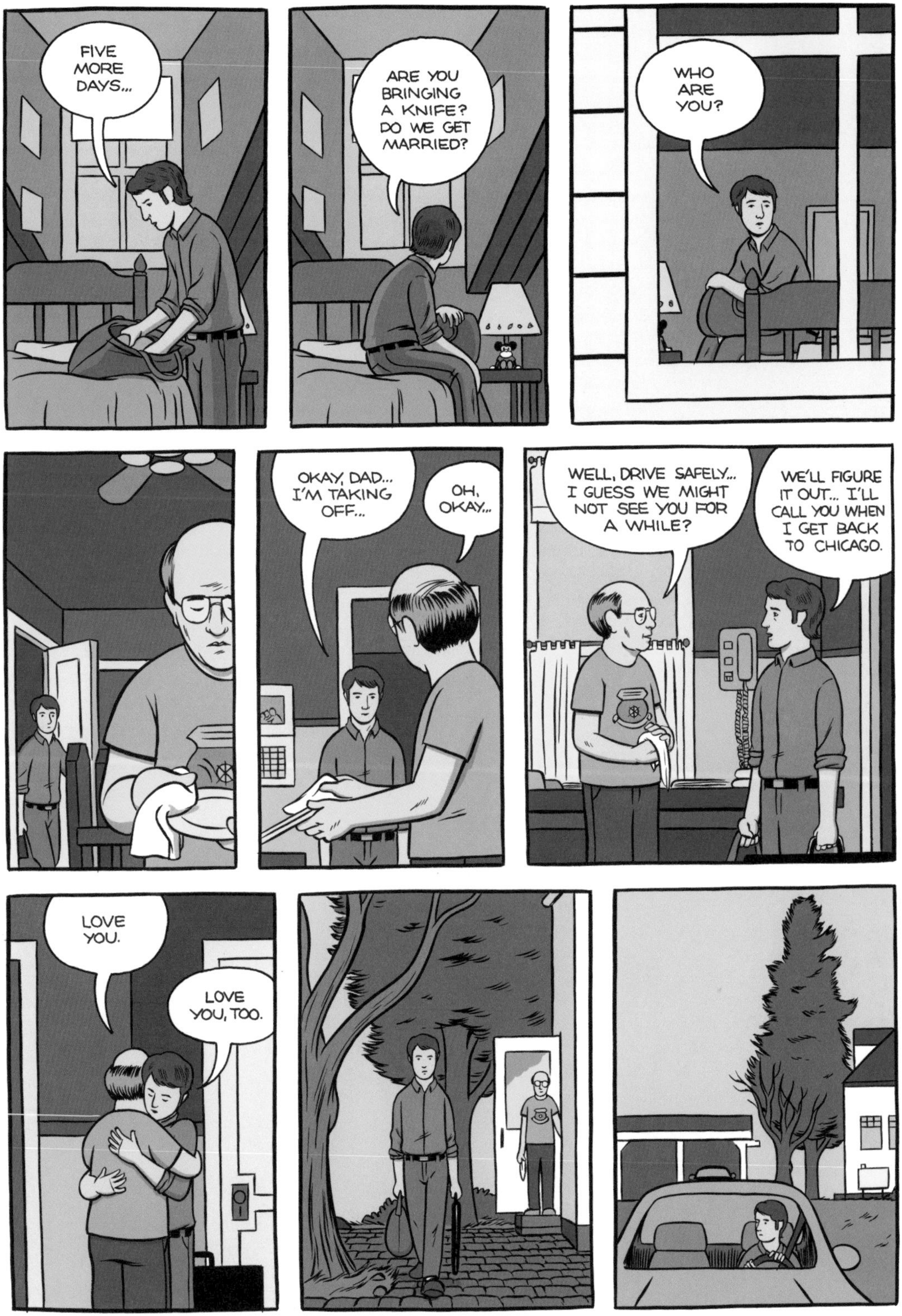
FIVE MORE DAYS...
ARE YOU BRINGING A KNIFE? DO WE GET MARRIED?
WHO ARE YOU?
OKAY, DAD... I'M TAKING OFF...
OH, OKAY...
WELL, DRIVE SAFELY... I GUESS WE MIGHT NOT SEE YOU FOR A WHILE?
WE'LL FIGURE IT OUT... I'LL CALL YOU WHEN I GET BACK TO CHICAGO.
LOVE YOU.
LOVE YOU, TOO.

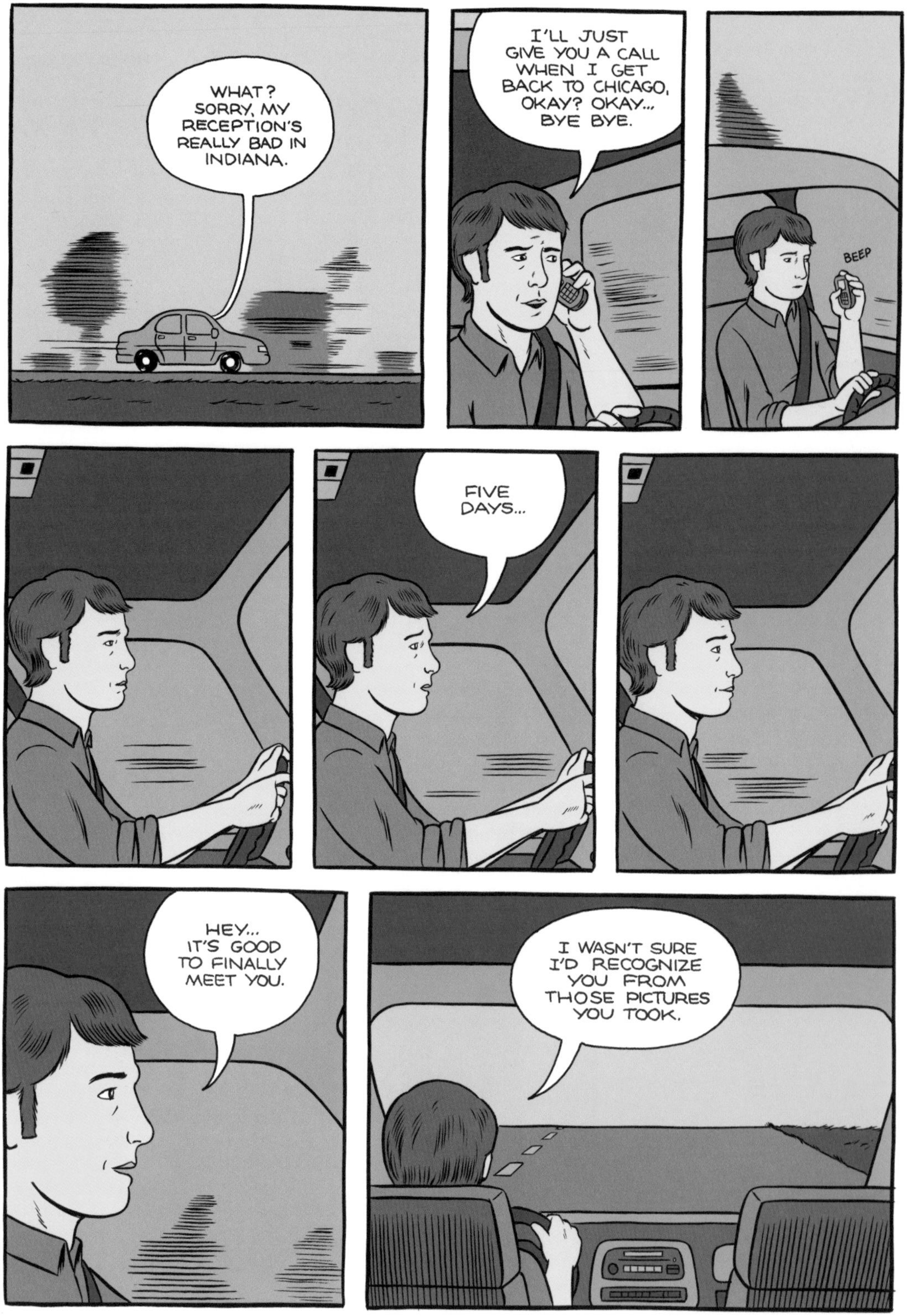
WHAT? SORRY, MY RECEPTION'S REALLY BAD IN INDIANA.
I'LL JUST GIVE YOU A CALL WHEN I GET BACK TO CHICAGO, OKAY? OKAY... BYE BYE.
BEEP
FIVE DAYS...
HEY... IT'S GOOD TO FINALLY MEET YOU.
I WASN'T SURE I'D RECOGNIZE YOU FROM THOSE PICTURES YOU TOOK.

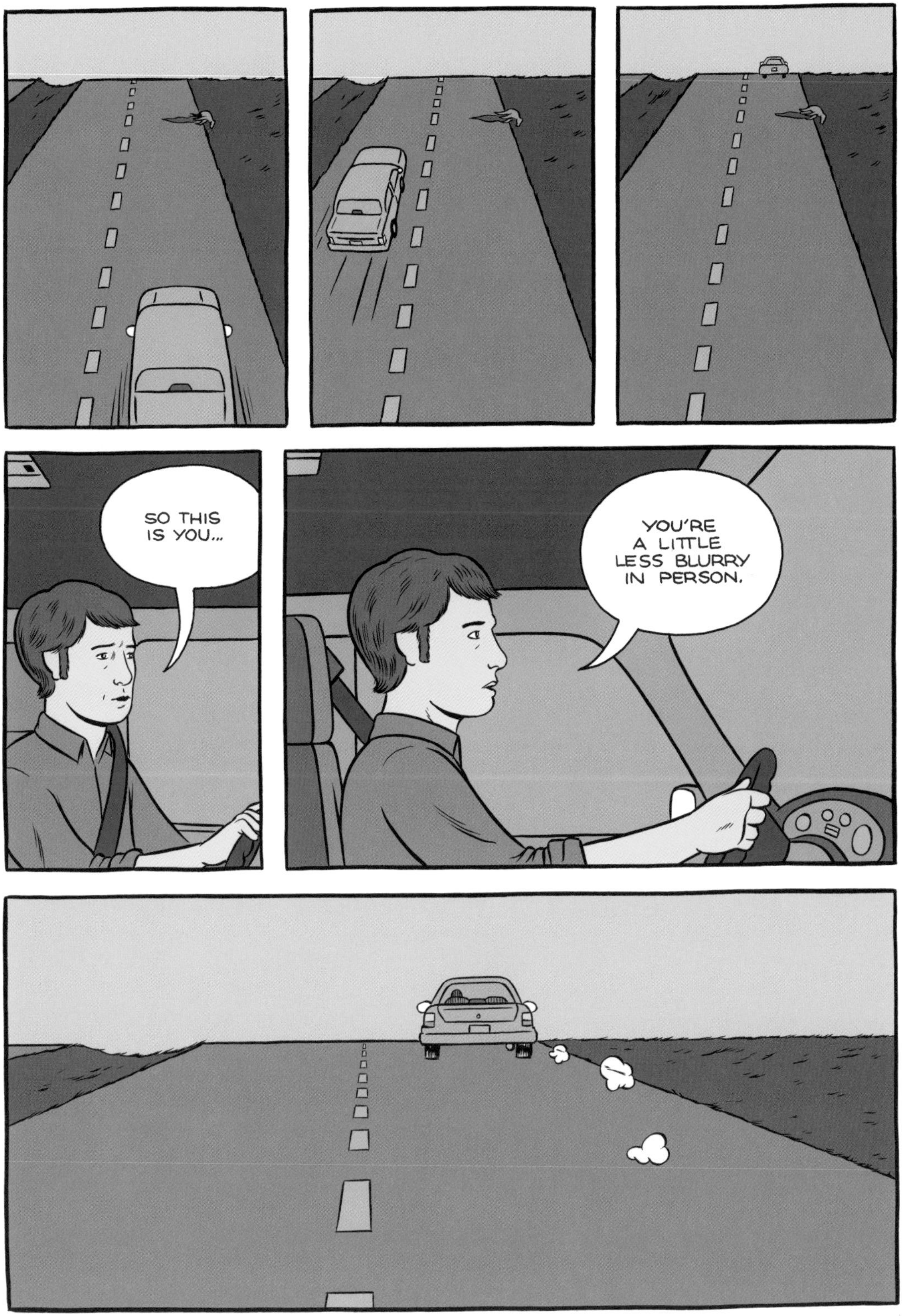
SO THIS IS YOU...
YOU'RE A LITTLE LESS BLURRY IN PERSON.

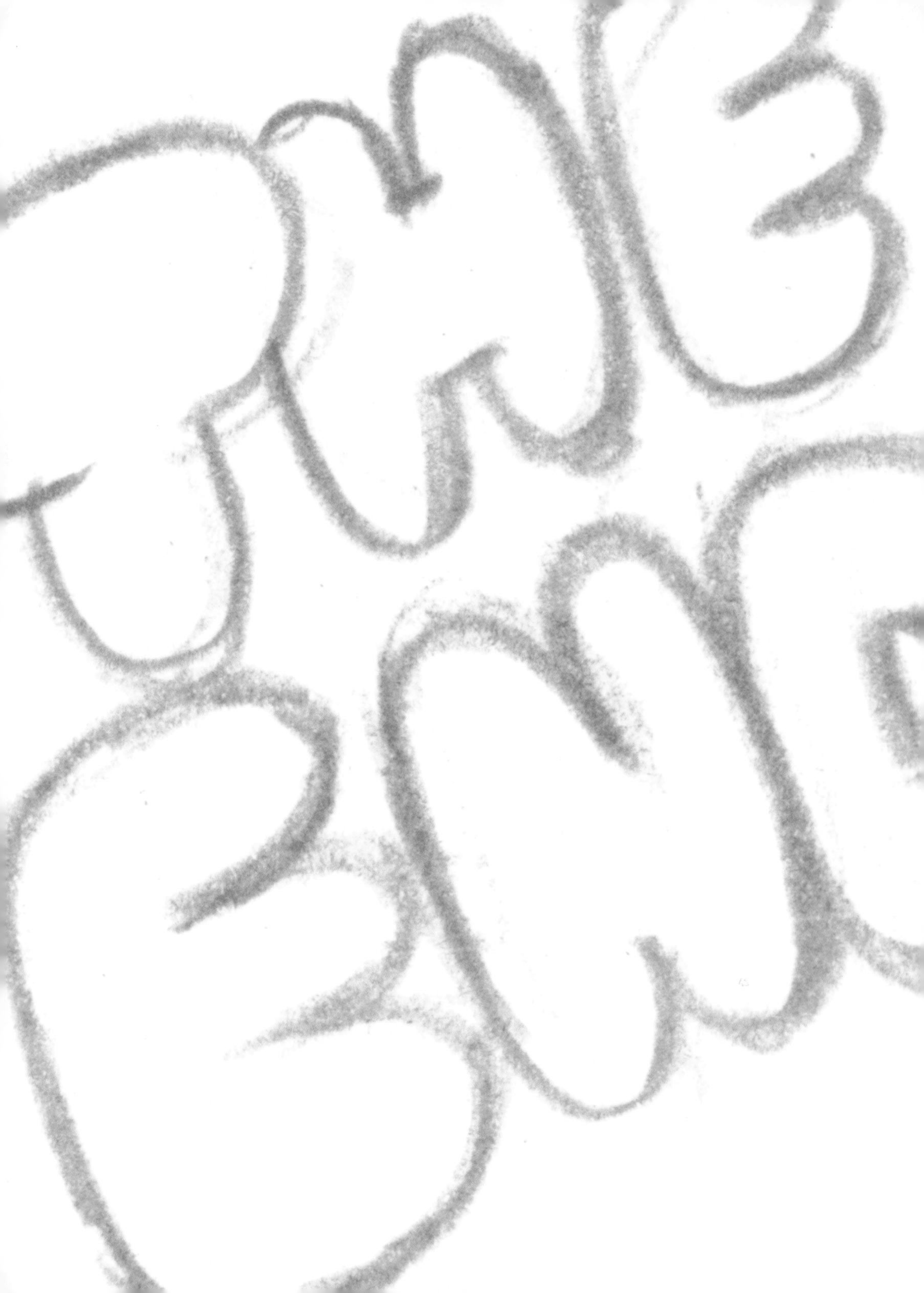

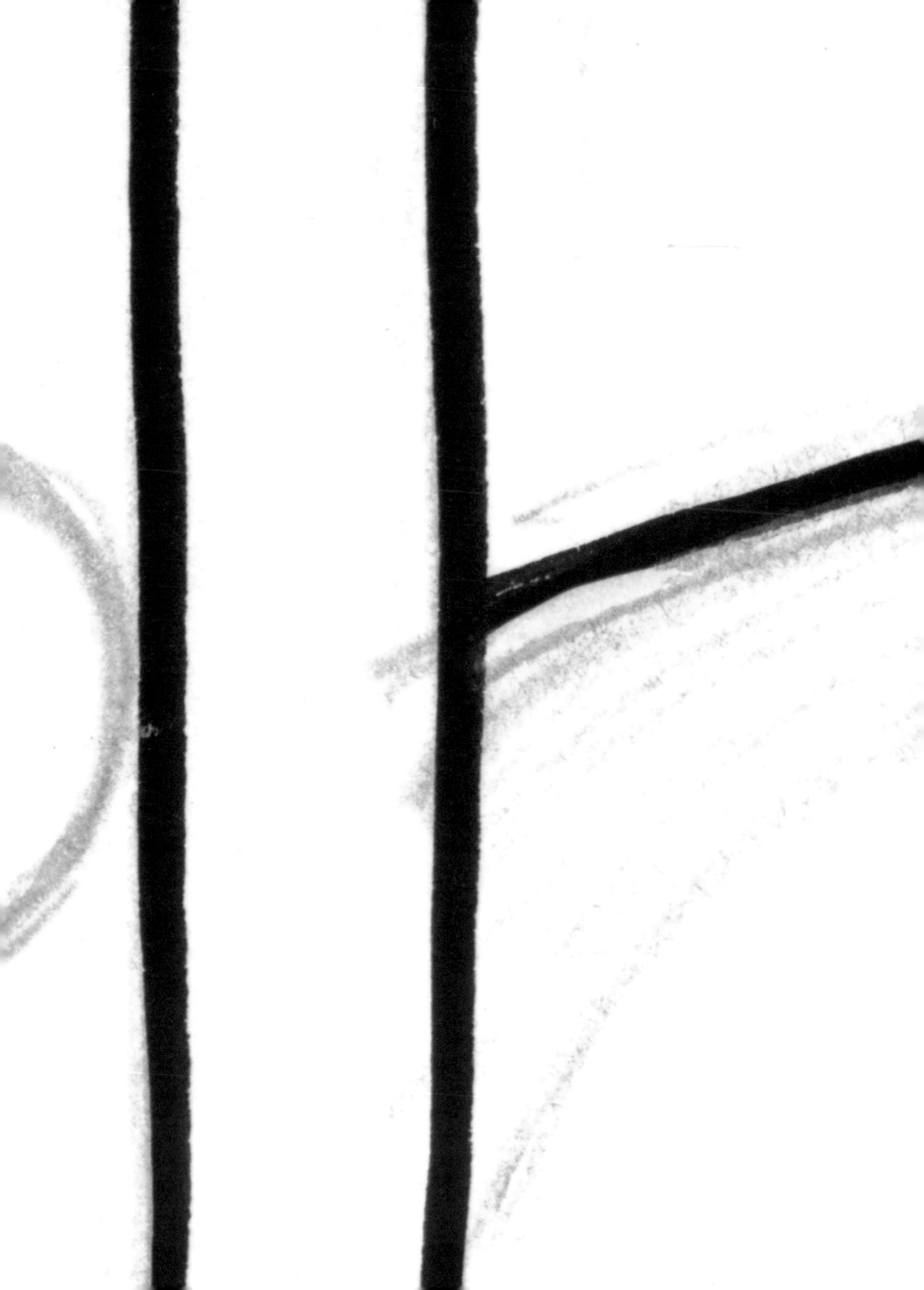

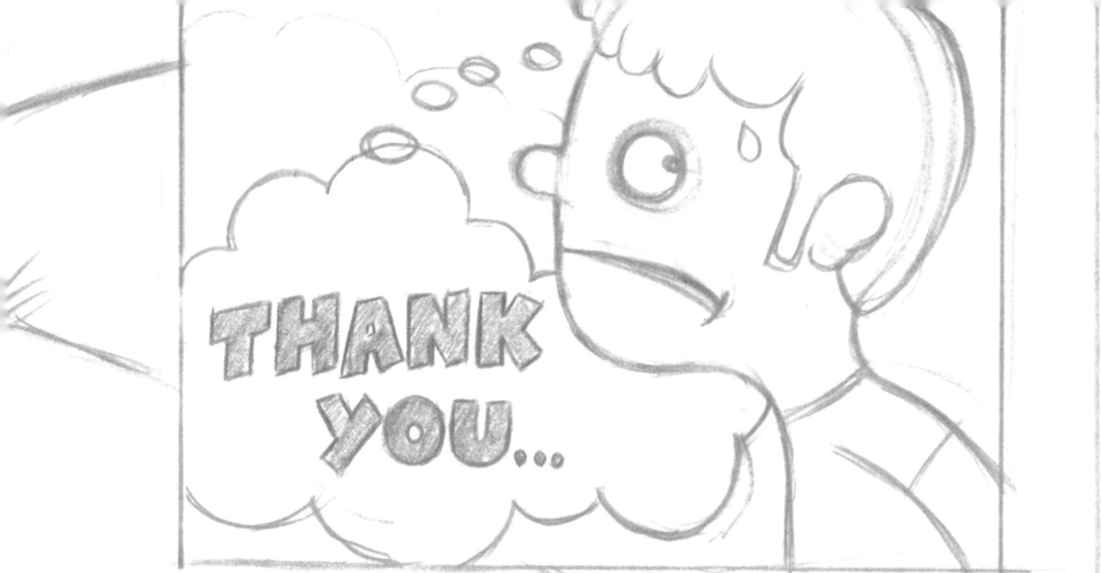
THANK YOU...

TO KIM THOMPSON AND GARY GROTH FOR THEIR INEXHAUSTIBLE PATIENCE WITH THIS VOLUME (AND AUTHOR), TO ERIC REYNOLDS FOR TIRELESS SHEPHERDING, TO DIANA SCHUTZ FOR HER FRIENDSHIP AND FOR "AUTOBIOGRAPHIX," WHICH SERVED AS PARTIAL INSPIRATION FOR THIS VOLUME,

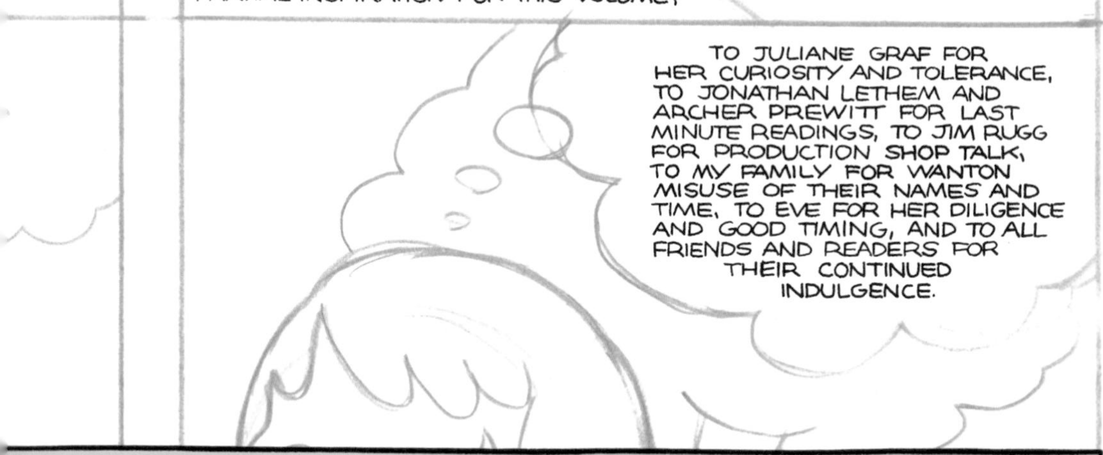

TO JULIANE GRAF FOR HER CURIOSITY AND TOLERANCE, TO JONATHAN LETHEM AND ARCHER PREWITT FOR LAST MINUTE READINGS, TO JIM RUGG FOR PRODUCTION SHOP TALK, TO MY FAMILY FOR WANTON MISUSE OF THEIR NAMES AND TIME, TO EVE FOR HER DILIGENCE AND GOOD TIMING, AND TO ALL FRIENDS AND READERS FOR THEIR CONTINUED INDULGENCE.

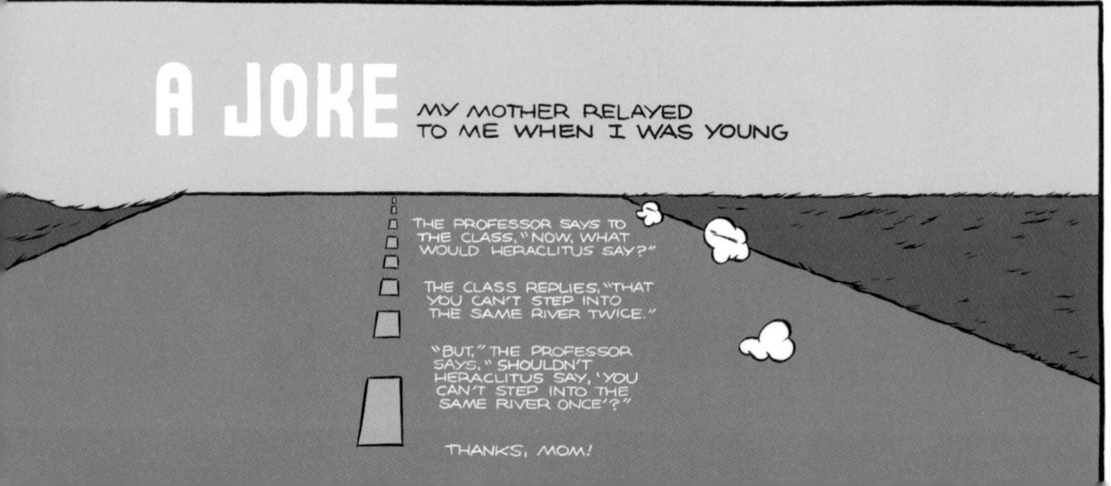
A JOKE
MY MOTHER RELAYED TO ME WHEN I WAS YOUNG
THE PROFESSOR SAYS TO THE CLASS, "NOW, WHAT WOULD HERACLITUS SAY?"
THE CLASS REPLIES, "THAT YOU CAN'T STEP INTO THE SAME RIVER TWICE."
"BUT," THE PROFESSOR SAYS, "SHOULDN'T HERACLITUS SAY, 'YOU CAN'T STEP INTO THE SAME RIVER ONCE'?"
THANKS, MOM!

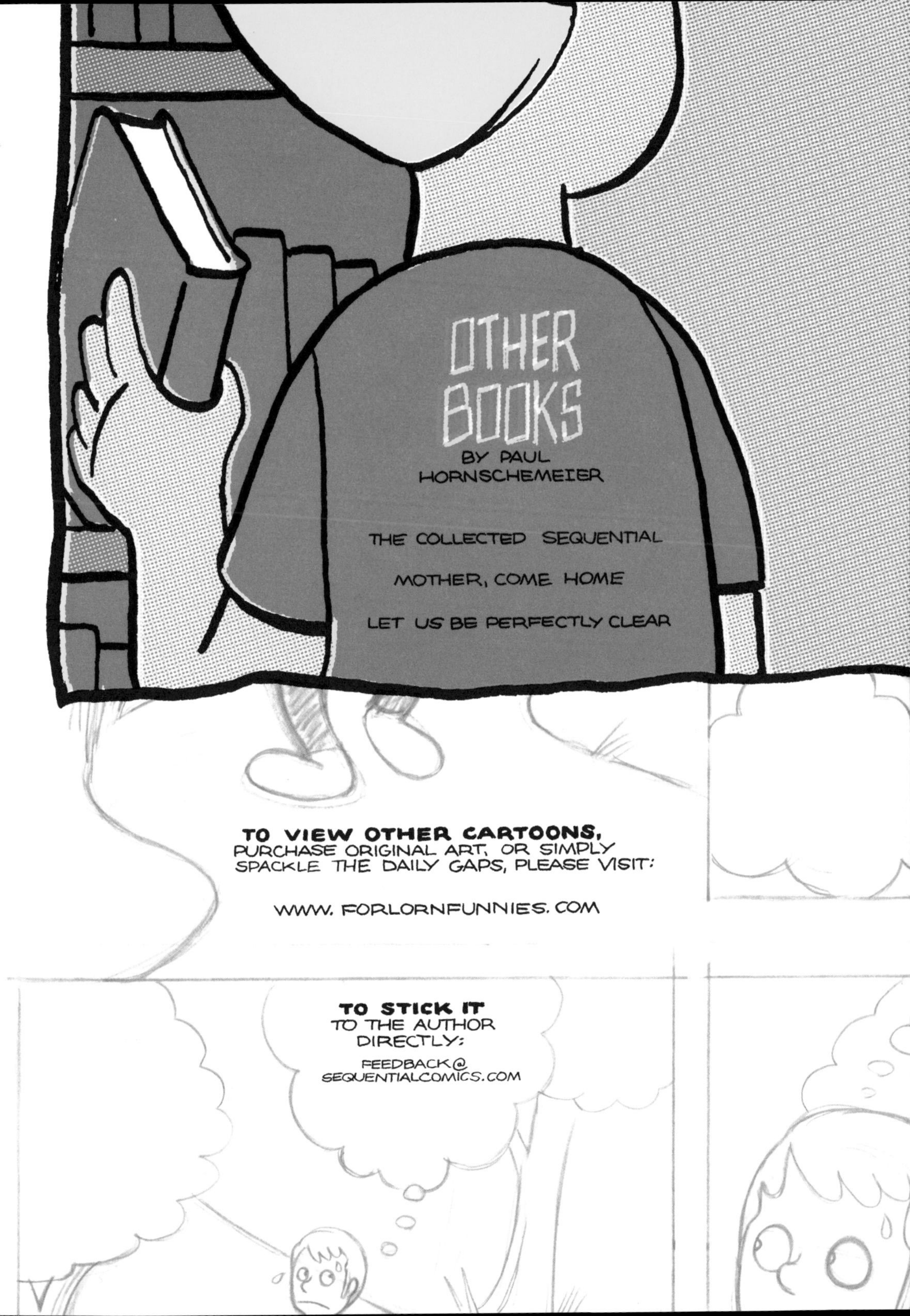
OTHER BOOKS
BY PAUL HORNSCHEMEIER
THE COLLECTED SEQUENTIAL
MOTHER, COME HOME
LET US BE PERFECTLY CLEAR
TO VIEW OTHER CARTOONS, PURCHASE ORIGINAL ART, OR SIMPLY SPACKLE THE DAILY GAPS, PLEASE VISIT:
WWW. FORLORNFUNNIES. COM
TO STICK IT TO THE AUTHOR DIRECTLY:
FEEDBACK@ SEQUENTIALCOMICS.COM

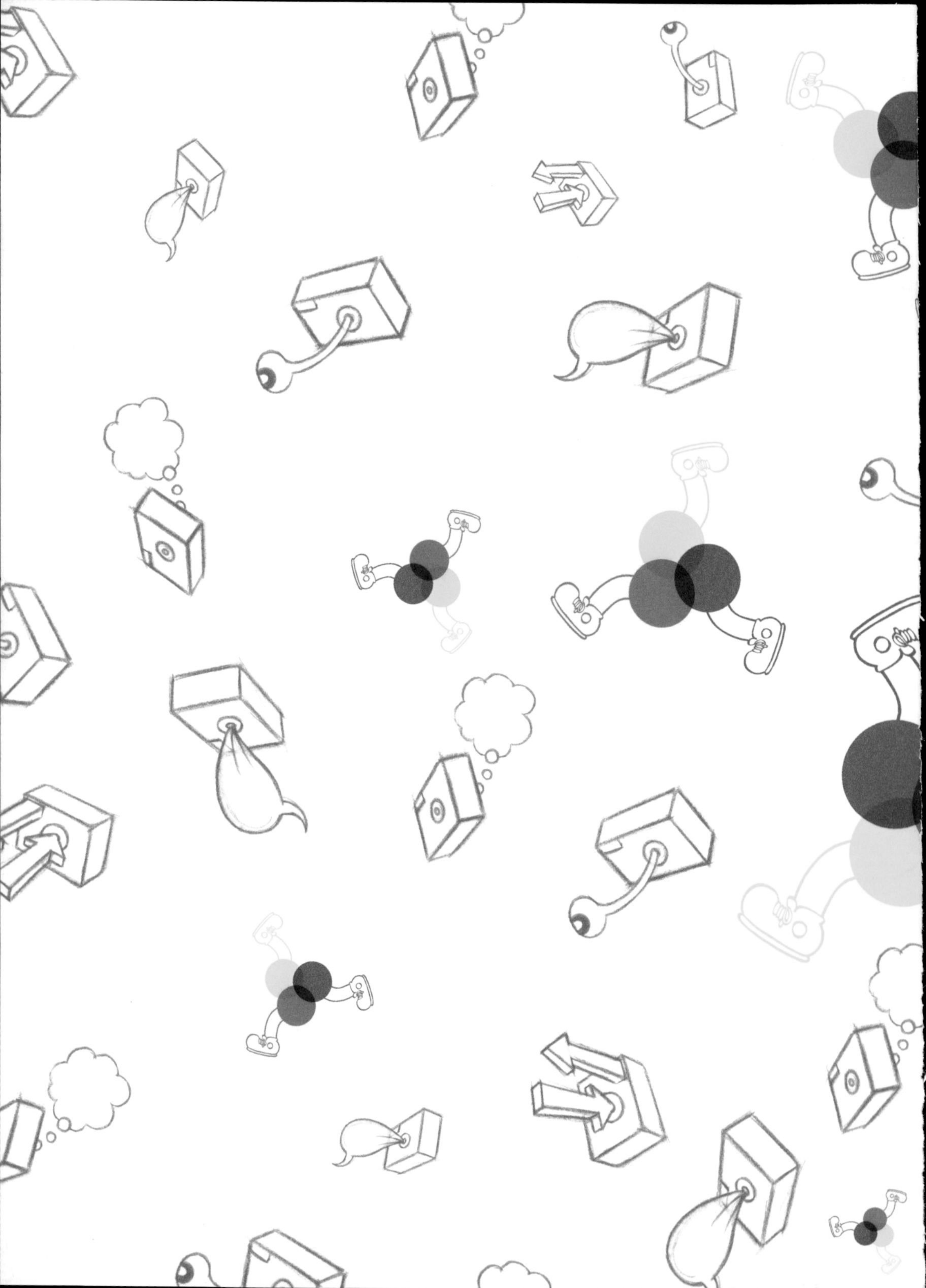